PROSPECT AND REFUGE IN THE LANDSCAPE OF JANE AUSTEN

To Paul

Prospect and Refuge in the Landscape of Jane Austen

BARBARA BRITTON WENNER
The University of Cincinnati, USA

ASHGATE

© Barbara Britton Wenner 2006

All rights reserved. No part of this publication may be reproduced, stored in a retrieval system, or transmitted in any form or by any means, electronic, mechanical, photocopying, recording, or otherwise without the prior permission of the publisher.

Barbara Britton Wenner has asserted her moral right under the Copyright, Designs and Patents Act, 1988, to be identified as the author of this work.

Published by
Ashgate Publishing Limited
Wey Court East
Union Road
Farnham
Surrey, GU9 7PT
England

Ashgate Publishing Company
110 Cherry Street
Suite 3-1
Burlington
VT 05401-3818
USA

Ashgate website: http://www.ashgate.com

British Library Cataloguing in Publication Data
Wenner, Barbara Britton
  Prospect and refuge in the landscape of Jane Austen
  1.Austen, Jane, 1775–1817—Settings 2.Austen, Jane, 1775–1817—Homes and haunts 3.Austen, Jane, 1775–1817—Criticism and interpretation 4.Landscape in literature 5.Geography in literature
  I.Title
  823.7

Library of Congress Cataloging-in-Publication Data
Wenner, Barbara Britton, 1946–
  Prospect and refuge in the landscape of Jane Austen / Barbara Britton Wenner.
    p. cm.
  Includes bibliographical references and index.
  ISBN 0-7546-5178-9 (alk. paper)
  1. Austen, Jane, 1775–1817—Settings. 2. Women and literature—England—History—19th century. 3. Austen, Jane, 1775–1817—Characters—Heroines. 4. Austen, Jane, 1775–1817—Knowledge—Geography. 5. Personal space in literature. 6. Landscape in literature. 7. Heroines in literature. 8. Setting (Literature) I. Title.

PR4038.S46W46 2005
823'.7—dc22

2005011870

Transferred to Digital Printing in 2011

ISBN 978-0-7546-5178-9

Printed and bound in Great Britain by Printondemand-worldwide.com

Contents

List of Figures		*vii*
Preface		*ix*
Acknowledgements		*xv*
1	An Introduction to the Landscape of Jane Austen	1
2	The Potential of Death by Landscape	13
3	"Four White Cows Disposed at Equal Distances"—or—Steel Traps to Bowers in Austen's Short Fiction	31
4	Heroines-in-Training: The First Three	41
5	Enclaves of Civility amidst Clamorous Impertinence	63
6	The Geography of *Persuasion*	83
7	*Sanditon*: Half Topography, Half Romance	103
8	Some Nineteenth-Century Reactions, Twenty-First Century Women in the Landscape and Final Remarks	111
Bibliography		*117*
Index		*121*

List of Figures

2.1 Thomas Gainsborough, "Cottage Door." Courtesy of Huntington Library, Art Collections, and Botanical Gardens.   22

3.1 Thomas Gainsborough, "Mr. and Mrs. Andrews," (1748-50). Courtesy National Gallery. Bought with contributions from the Pilgrim Trust, the National Art Collections Fund, Associated Television Ltd, and Mr. and Mrs. W. W. Spooner, 1960.   37

4.1 Humphry Repton, "Mr. Repton's Opinion of the Aspects," *Red Book Ferne Hall*. Courtesy of Pierpont Morgan Library, New York. Gift of Mr. Junius S. Morgan and Mr. Henry Morgan, 1954.17. Photography: Joseph Zehavi.   46

4.2 Samuel Palmer. "View from Rook's Hill, Kent" (1843). Courtesy of Yale Center for British Art. Paul Mellon Collection.   51

6.1 Thomas Gainsborough, "Haymaker and Sleeping Girl." Courtesy of Museum of Fine Arts, Boston. M. Theresa B. Hopkins Fund and Seth K. Sweetser Fund. 53.2553.   90

Preface

Recently, I had the pleasure of experiencing Jane Austen's landscape myself. After renting a car in Winchester, my spouse and I set out to explore Hampshire. Our final destination that first day was Selborne, where we were to stay in a 500-year-old thatched-roof cottage. Even though the sun was low in the sky, I felt drawn from the main road and toward Chawton, about four miles from Selborne. Suddenly, after passing a dozen cottages or so, there it was—Chawton Cottage, Jane Austen's home for the last eight years of her life. A plain red brick, two-story cottage, it glowed in the late day sun and promised more pleasure of looking at the landscape during our visit.

Focusing upon Jane Austen's landscape—the ways readers perceive it, the ways her heroines regarded it, and the ways Jane Austen herself interpreted the land around her aesthetically—increases our awareness of the power of the natural environment in her work. Here we will examine some theories of aesthetic geography, the evolving ways in which Jane Austen describes her fictional landscape and the landscapes she knew personally. We will attempt to understand how Jane Austen's heroines used their surroundings to grow in their knowledge of society and themselves.

The next day we returned to visit Chawton Cottage (now officially called Jane Austen House Museum), a rather imposing house for a "cottage,"[1] with six bedrooms and large Georgian sash windows which allow a generous amount of light to stream into the rooms. Located on the formerly busy Winchester/Guildford Road, the cottage occupied a very public spot in Jane Austen's day, unlike its location on the quiet road today where all of the traffic has been diverted one-half mile north on the heavily traveled A31. Although the house is frequently photographed from the garden, actually seeing its close proximity to the once-busy road in front makes the viewer acutely aware of how noisy this location must have been during the early nineteenth century. However, now Chawton has become a sleepy village with many picturesque thatched-roof houses, the Grey Friar, a pub with a picture of Jane over the fireplace, and a tearoom, appropriately named Cassandra's Cup, with a view of Jane Austen's house directly across the road.

Even though her brother, Edward Knight, who owned the cottage, thoughtfully had the window directly on the busy road bricked up, Jane Austen still had plenty of passers-by and visitors due to the location of the cottage. According to Jane Austen's letters, the garden at Chawton Cottage, with its shrubbery walk on the border, gave Jane an excuse for outdoor activity. Less than one-half mile from her home stands Chawton Manor House (now restored and containing an extensive

---

[1] Jane Austen herself was never known to refer to her Chawton *home* as a cottage.

collection of books by early British women writers), one of the residences her brother, Edward, had inherited from his adoptive parents, the Knights. Jane Austen visited other parts of England, from Bath to Lyme Regis to Southampton and her brother's estate, Godmersham, in Kent, but Chawton became the place where she revised her first three novels and wrote her last three. The area around it must have had a significant effect on her landscape descriptions.

Because of my own interest in this landscape, I immediately sought out the footpaths Jane Austen had walked, knowing that many of these paths had been in place from time immemorial. An intricate and extensive network of footpaths exists throughout Hampshire. The first footpath we tried began near Gracious Street in Selborne. This footpath crossed a fence, using a stile—a wooden step up over the fence—then traversed a field to a chalky cliff of three-hundred-year-old beech trees overlooking the village and the Wakes, the estate of Gilbert White, well-known late eighteenth-century naturalist. This ancient grove of trees is known as the Hanger because of the way the beeches lean over the three-hundred-foot chalk scarp-face. Since this footpath is so near Chawton, Austen, an enthusiastic walker, surely traversed it on her way to the Selborne Fair. From this footpath, we had wonderful sheltered views of the Hampshire countryside, in fact, the same view Jane Austen would have had, overlooking the slightly rolling fields toward Chawton and Alton beyond. This footpath exemplifies what aesthetic geographer Jay Appleton might call "a good place to hide and a good place to seek" for someone like Jane Austen. She wanted to see the broader picture of the landscape and yet maintain her privacy there.

Across the street from Jane Austen House Museum, another promising footpath caught our eyes. This footpath went from the village between two hedges so close that they grazed our shoulders as we passed between them, over several turnstiles through a field where horses grazed. As we followed the muddy path through a wood, we came to a series of farm buildings and a diversion, marked by a sign, as the footpath continued through a field of cattle. A diversion is meant to be temporary until the farmer has made the necessary improvements requiring it. The footpaths through private property are always open for public use, but walkers also know that they must keep to the paths and always close any gates they open. We remembered Mr. Knightley's assiduous care for the public footpaths running through his property in *Emma*. He speaks to his brother, "I was telling you of my idea of moving the path to Langham, of turning it more to the right that it may not cut through the home meadows ... I should not attempt it, if it were the means of inconvenience to the Highbury people" (128). Even today, the English people give legal protection to footpaths and enjoy walking on them.

If we examine how topography affected Jane Austen and how she related to her landscape, we notice that in many ways, her relationship with her environment parallels her heroines' relationship with the landscape in her narratives. She had very public access to society, both in living directly on the main road to Winchester and following the footpaths that crisscross the area around her home. Though she had good opportunities for what aesthetic geographers call "prospect-viewing," from the beech hanger to the narrow hedgerows with views out onto the fields, to the large windows overlooking the coach route, she also had recourse to a private refuge. A "zone of safety," as Appleton might call it, provided her with a retreat when she desired it, both to stay out of the picture herself as well as to write her heroines into it.

A short walk from Jane Austen's cottage brought us to Chawton Manor House. Some have thought Jane Austen wrote many of her novels there, but that seems unlikely as the house had either tenants or the numerous family members occupying it while she lived in Chawton. However, she may have being thinking of Chawton Manor House as she wrote about Donwell Abbey in *Emma*. We walked, as Emma might have, "to the delicious shade of a short avenue of limes, which stretching beyond the garden ... seemed to finish the pleasure grounds" (355). Neither ruined abbey nor a river here, but certainly the view of the distant fields beyond the garden and the avenue of limes made Chawton Manor House reminiscent of Austen's novelistic landscapes. The ancient-looking lime walk that provides a vista toward the house itself was planted after Jane Austen's death; the seemingly ancient steps and walls behind the house were built around 1895, I was surprised (and maybe a little disappointed) to learn. Even the walled garden on the property had been started in 1818, a year after Jane Austen's death. However, the old ha-ha has been excavated, a reminder of the uninterrupted "proprietary" prospect from the house toward the open fields beyond, and the other approaches around the house, including the location of the church and graveyard, remain as they were during Jane Austen's time.

Because Jane Austen spent most of her life about twenty miles away from Chawton in Steventon, we decided to join the Jane Austen Society in attending Evensong at St. Nicholas Church there. We followed the same narrow track to the church that the Austens had followed from George Austen's rectory. Although the rectory no longer exists, we saw the site of the manse, along with the nettle patch marking the pump that had been near the house. The church remains nearly as it had been when it was built in the twelfth century, a thousand-year-old yew standing next to it. This landscape has been sentimentalized by Austen relatives as "picturesque," as biographer David Nokes writes, using "memories which unconsciously refashion the landscape into a topographical metaphor for Austen's art" (56). Jane Austen herself "left us no delicious Proustian memories of the rectory's magical garden." Nokes claims she found in "the rural isolation of Steventon implied privation rather than pastoral contentment" (58). However, I believe she appreciated the "small and unassuming beauties" of the place that her nephew later described in his *Memoir* (18).

The following day we traveled to Lyme Regis on the Devon coast (two and one-half hours from Chawton by car). As we came nearer the coast, the roads narrowed and became steeper. Soon, our car was scraping both sides of twenty-foot high hedgerows. The weather was rainy and cool, until just before we reached Lyme Regis, when the skies became blue and the stiff Lyme Bay breeze blew in so warm we had to remove our jackets. The Cobb, a large stone seawall, goes hundreds of yards out into the sea. It is the only way of protecting boats at Lyme Regis, which is flanked by high blue lias and golden sandstone cliffs and a shingle beach, the stones cracking like pistols when the tide comes in. I kept looking for Granny's Teeth. About two-thirds of the way to the end of the breakwater, I saw some slippery, roundish stones, going up the wall (twenty to thirty feet) with no way of holding on—so precarious, I could not summon the courage to go all the way to the top.

This landscape is so exposed that it fits with Appleton's formal geographic definition of hazard—"an incident or condition prejudicial to the attainment of comfort, safety or survival" (269). Louisa Musgrove, in falling off the "Teeth," did not possess sufficient knowledge of hazards and respect for them, and here, reliance upon even the most competent of men, Captain Wentworth, was of no use. Louisa was saved by a cool-headed woman, Anne, who was well aware of female vulnerability in the landscape and who coolly organized the members of the community into a rescue party. Anne had a knowledge and respect for hazards and knew not to expose herself to such a hazard as Granny's Teeth.

The Cobb is a great contrast to the next landscape at Lyme Regis that we visited. We walked across the beach from the Cobb to Lyme Regis itself. From there, we followed the directions in Anne-Marie Edwards' *In the Steps of Jane Austen*. The route led us up to Charmouth fields and to the Coastal Trail. Here on the footpath we were back to the sheltered zone-of-safety geography where Jane Austen felt so comfortable walking when she visited Lyme Regis herself in 1804. Sometimes called an "interface" by Appleton, this spot between the woods and the coastal cliffs becomes "the zone of contact between those parts of the environment which are visible from a vantage-point and those which are not, or between prospect-dominant and refuge-dominant areas" (269). This is how Jane Austen describes the scene in *Persuasion*:

> The scenes in this neighborhood, Charmouth, with its high grounds and extensive sweeps of country, and still more its sweet retired bay, backed by dark cliffs, where fragments of low rock among the sands make it the happiest spot for watching the flow of the tide, for sitting in unwearied contemplation ... these places must be visited and visited again, to make the worth of Lyme understood. (117)

This view is aptly described by Austen herself when she writes that "all must linger and gaze on a first return to the sea, whoever deserve to look on it at all" (*Persuasion* 117). As we stood at the top of Charmouth fields footpath, we had shelter as well as a good overview of the entire town, the Cobb, and a long stretch of seacoast. We proceeded beside the Lyme, a little stream going down to the bay, on a path sheltered by a tunnel of trees and hedges.

A short train trip from Winchester brought us to one of the most frequently mentioned landscapes of Jane Austen's novels: Bath. Austen scholar Irene Collins describes Bath in the 1790s:

> Bath was one of the architectural wonders of western Europe. Visitors who knew what they were about would pause as they approached the city over Kingsdown Hill and view the honey-coloured spectacle before them with suitable rapture. Jane could not help be impressed, even though her arrival on both her early visits took place in rain. (178)

Little evidence exists that Jane Austen worked on any of her fiction, besides the fragment *The Watsons*, during her stays in Bath, but Bath provides landscapes for both *Northanger Abbey* and *Persuasion*, and numerous allusions to the city are found in most of her works. On May 17, 1799, Jane wrote to Cassandra: "The prospect from the Drawing room window at which I now write is rather picturesque as it commands a perspective veiw [sic] of the left side of Brock Street, broken by three Lombardy poplars in the Garden of the last house in Queen's Parade" (41). Bath is a city of crescent after crescent of stone townhouses and many scenic overlooks. Beechen Hill provides a perfect place for Henry Tilney's discourse on "foregrounds, distances, and second distances—sidescreens and perspectives— lights and shades" as well as Catherine Morland's rejection of the city itself as "unworthy to make part of a landscape" (94). Bath is both of these—the ideal prospect and a gray sea of buildings. Of course, shops and entertainment enough (both in the nineteenth and the twenty-first centuries) abound to distract many nature lovers, but Bath has riverine valleys and hilly terrain, an ideal setting for the beautiful crescents with broad expanses of grass, and footpaths, both into the hills surrounding Bath and along the Bristol-Avon Canal. Bath allowed eighteenth-century visitors to have the comforts of a city and the verdant and varied landscape of the country.

We arrived at Bath Spa and took a footpath that runs along the top of a hill overlooking the city, less than a mile from the former Austen residence at 4 Sydney Place. This landscape was open—no hedgerows—and gave us remarkable views of many terraces of houses—crescents on the hills on the other side of the valley and the woods above them. Yet, the path itself was protected by trees, and the walker could remain fairly sheltered. Surely, Jane Austen too had taken this path, which proceeded down to the Bristol-Avon Canal (constructed during the time Jane Austen lived in Bath). We followed the path down to the canal and then along the towpath, which eventually went through the place where Sydney Gardens had been—just opposite 4 Sydney Place.

From her residence in Bath, Jane Austen easily walked out in the country, looked back upon the city, and boated (as we did) on the Bristol Avon River to Bathampton Mill. Like us, she enjoyed the open green spaces in front of the Royal Crescent and the park near Pulteney Bridge. We moved quickly and easily from the public, wide-open green space of the Royal Crescent to the narrow Gravel Walk, which follows along behind the gardens and fences of townhouses near the Circus. Jane Austen appropriately chose this secluded landscape as the one where Anne Elliot and Captain Wentworth came to know each other's true feelings. Bath provided a wonderful novelistic landscape to move characters quickly from distractingly busy Milson Street, lined with interesting shops, to the Upper Assembly Rooms, to those open, wind-blown fields above Bath.

Finally, we journeyed to Box Hill, a seventy-five minute trip by car from Chawton today. From Emma's fictive Highbury, the trip was seven miles by carriage. As I recalled the Box Hill picnic from *Emma*, I became increasingly aware that the trip must have been quite a large undertaking, worthy of being called an expedition, and the participants must have been worn out when they reached the top of the highest summit in southern England. No wonder Frank Churchill's chattering was so irritated and irritating. The trip, even today, seemed to me a long, circuitous uphill journey. But once at the summit, we were confronted with two views: on one side Dorking and all of south Surrey, on the other side a confusing tangle of woods, difficult to follow and find one's way around—what Appleton might call "contraposition," or "the juxtaposition of symbols of contrasting type" (268).

Was this landscape "prospect" or "refuge"? The scene in *Emma* appears confused and confusing on that point, and as the narrator tells us, "There seemed a principle of separation ... too strong for any fine prospects" (361). I am reminded of what narratologist Mieke Bal says about such a landscape: "A special role may be played by the boundary between two opposed locations" and "it is possible to be trapped in such places" (45). Emma certainly seems trapped by her own words at the Box Hill picnic. Could it be that the landscape had a role in it? They "looked without seeing—admired without intelligence" (361). It is certainly a strange trap in which Emma finds herself at Box Hill. She fails in her attempts to transgress and to transform this landscape. In the end, Emma needs Mr. Knightley's corrective reminders to understand the true importance of what transpires in this landscape. Seeing Box Hill as the exploring party in *Emma* may have seen it suggested to me the social, physical, and cultural importance of landscape and the complex ways in which they interact in Jane Austen's fiction.

    The preceding pages chronicle my personal experience in the landscapes where Jane Austen lived and visited. I wanted to understand (even with the changes of two centuries) how the landscape might have been seen and enjoyed by Austen, and, by extension, her heroines. Now we will move from a brief experience of reading of what still remains today of Austen's landscapes toward a reading of Jane Austen's fictive landscape.

Acknowledgements

Portions of this study are based on articles that previously appeared in volumes 23 and 24 of *Persuasions: The Journal of the Jane Austen Society* and in volume 8 of *The European Romantic Review*. I am grateful to Laurie Kaplan and Regina Hewett for permission to use this material.

I am grateful to the University of Cincinnati for grants that supported my research. I wish to acknowledge with gratitude the help I received from David Venturo, Professor at the College of New Jersey, and the late Robin Sheets, former Director of Women's Studies at the University of Cincinnati, as I began my work with Jane Austen in graduate school.

Special thanks go to my friends and colleagues who encouraged me along the way: Louise Flavin, Marlene Miner, Rhonda Pettit, Tami Phenix and Alison Russell. I should also like to thank Janet Reed for reading drafts of my manuscript and giving her invaluable criticism. Without Janet's help, I am not sure I would have completed this study.

I appreciate the support and encouragement of the Jane Austen Society of North America, especially of members Martha Caprarotta and Robert Benson, and also the help I received while in England from the Jane Austen Society there and particularly Michael Davis. I am grateful as well to the J. P. Morgan Library for the assistance I received in my research and the Yale Center for British Art. Financial support from the Charles Phelps Taft Memorial Fund at the University of Cincinnati has also been much appreciated.

I wish to express thanks for all the cheerful and willing assistance I received from Ashgate editor Ann Donahue.

Finally, I thank my daughter, Susan Wenner Jackson, for helping me copy edit my manuscript, and my husband Paul for his constant support and encouragement during the years I have spent on this project.

Chapter 1

An Introduction to the Landscape of Jane Austen

Readers of Jane Austen's novels might wonder how an entire book could be written about her landscapes. They might question how many of her landscapes are as fully described as those of later novelists such as Charles Dickens or Thomas Hardy, who were capable of painting quite particularized scenes. Novelists many times use landscape extensively, not only to establish a sense of place but also to allow readers actually to picture a location in detail. Austen's landscapes are not detailed. No travelogue visions of the south of France or Italy ever appear in her novels. Her landscape descriptions are few and spare, requiring some imagination on the reader's part to picture the scenes—"dull elves" will be disappointed as they search for local color. Certainly many of her contemporary readers would have been more familiar than we are with the places where the novels were set and so would not need to know more than Austen writes about the scenes, but still her novels appeal to readers who have never visited England two-hundred years later. As she seldom completely describes her heroines, so she leaves much of the landscape for the readers to fill in for themselves. This gap between what is written and what might be imagined provides us as readers with expanded enjoyment every time we read an Austen novel, as we discover more facets both to the characters and to the landscape.[1] As well, Austen's lack of elaboration in her landscapes places an obligation on the reader to discover the importance of the scenes she does describe.

Austen did not discuss her use of landscape in fiction very much; however, readers might recognize some similarities between the ways two late twentieth-century women fiction writers approach landscape and Austen's own approach. In an attempt to understand what one woman writer is thinking as she conceptualizes her landscape, let us begin with the present day American novelist and short story writer, Annie Proulx, as she reflects on the importance of landscape in her work:

> The outsider's eye is a writer's stock-in-trade, a persistent effort to grasp events through place and season, or through nuances of intonation, language, rhythm, phraseology, or

---

[1] Although Austen's descriptions may not be as effusive as those of other authors of the period, she is extremely accurate in her placement of characters with their settings. In "The Architectural Setting of Jane Austen's Novels" (*Journal of the Warburg and Courtauld Institutes* 31 1968, 404-412), Nikolaus Pevsner describes in great detail the places where various characters lived in Bath and London (including helpful maps). Most of the places in those cities are within walking distance of each other. Austen was personally acquainted with these places and situated her characters on streets which exactly matched their status. Camden Place, home of Sir Walter Elliot, is even located on "shaky ground," this a detail gleaned from a long-time Austen admirer and resident of Bath, Michael Davis.

through regional physical characteristics, climate and weather .... The characters in a story, like people in life, behave as their landscape makes them behave—what they eat and wear, the work they do, the thoughts they think ... When I write, I try to make landscapes rise from the page, to appear in the camera lens of the reader's mind. The reader is also an absent presence, but one that's leaning a sharp and influential elbow on my shoulder. (139)

Did Jane Austen think in the same way about landscape and how the reader would react to it? Of course, cameras had not been invented, but Austen was influenced by the framing device known as a Claude glass, a mirror which a viewer could use to place limitations on the view. Named after Claude Lorrain, whose landscapes were so popular with late eighteenth-century English art lovers, this hinged device the size of a lady's compact or a miniature book allowed the viewer to see the landscape as though it were a small painting. In many ways the Claude glass allowed the traveler to turn a real scene into art, with its associated frame and limited colors. The traveler then felt obligated to choose the culturally accepted scene and leave the unsightly peasants' hovels and highway potholes outside the frame.

If a character is armed with a Claude glass, the conventional notion that characters "behave as their landscape makes them behave" might actually be reversed: Landscapes behave the way the characters make them behave. People reproduce what *they* see as the "norms" in their surrounding geography. If they are gentlemen landowners, the nature of the estate reflects their self-confidence and dominance over the landscape. The ha-has, subtly hidden, long, deep ditches in the parkland, allow them to view their estate without the boundary of a fence between them and their cattle. If they are women, they are very often marginalized and must find other ways of challenging the patriarchal "naturalness" of the landscape. As geographer Tim Cresswell states, "Places are active forces in the reproduction of norms—in the definition of appropriate practice" (16), and "marginalized events question the naturalness and absoluteness of assumed geographies" (149). So a clever tension may exist in literary landscape: the landscape influences the behavior of the characters, but characters, especially Jane Austen's heroines, find ways of challenging the landscape and finding new meaning there. The questioning of cultural assumptions, learning from liminal locations, and recognizing landscape as critical "agent" are all strongly evident in all of Jane Austen's fiction.

The importance of understanding the landscape, behaving as the landscape suggests, or finding ways to control the landscape (if that helps the heroine find her "self") is central to such present-day women writers as Annie Proulx and Canadian Margaret Atwood. When I think of the close attention to landscape and the position of women in *Close Range* by Proulx and *Wilderness Tips* by Atwood, I am reminded of their presence in Austen's work. This same "environmental imagination" comes into play throughout all of Austen's six novels, but it shows up even in her early writing and makes a strong mark on her final work, the fragment known as *Sanditon*. Margaret Atwood's narrator in "Death by Landscape," a short story from *Wilderness Tips*, tells the story of Lois, as she collects landscape paintings and remembers her girlfriend, Lucy, who disappeared years ago while they were hiking together: "She looks at the paintings, she looks into them. Every one of them is a picture of Lucy" (128). Lois retains an abnormal fascination with a wild Canadian landscape in which the figure and the ground shift in some very tricky ways.

Many questions came to my mind as I began to explore Jane Austen's use of landscape. How does Austen treat landscape differently than some women writers of the same period? How do Austen's heroines find a way to prevail in their environments? Along with these questions, how do Austen's heroines respond differently to the landscape than do the heroines of her closest male counterpart, novelist Sir Walter Scott? How do Austen's heroines make the landscape work in their behalf, whether listening in a hedgerow or finding spiritual rejuvenation in a bower? Can a heroine such as Fanny Price act as a "cure" in the ailing landscape of Mansfield Park? Everything in *Emma* is "only natural." What is natural? Does the landscape (and seascape as well) provide a place both to lose and to find self for the Austen heroine? And behind her protagonists, how is Austen herself using landscape to convey her meaning? The reader will find this writer's answers to the questions in the chapters that follow.

Austen had always taken an interest in geography. She remarked in a letter to her brother, Frank, in 1813, that she had been examining a map of Sweden (where he was then stationed) and "fancied it more like England than many other countries, many of the names have a strong resemblance to the English" (*Letters* 215). In a letter from 1814, as she critiqued her niece Anna's novelistic attempts, Jane Austen corrected Anna's geography, explaining that the characters "must be *two* days going from Dawlish to Bath; they are nearly 100 miles apart" (*Letters* 269).

As early as "Love and Freindship," Austen pokes fun at people who are "geographically impaired." In this story, a gentleman gets hopelessly lost trying to find his aunt's house, ending up at least 100 miles off course, although he "flatter[s] [himself] with being tolerably proficient in geography" (103). In Austen's last novel, *Persuasion*, Mrs. Musgrove is so ignorant that she cannot tell Bermuda from the Bahamas. These are, of course, examples of very tangible, physical geography, but concern arises as well for how a landscape makes a character feel or behave. In *Catharine,—Or The Bower*, when Camilla carelessly confuses Derbyshire and Yorkshire, her character is described as "shamefully ignorant as to the geography of England" (143). The primacy in Austen's mind of a sense of place establishes itself early.

This primacy of place, then, brings me to the aesthetic geographers. Here we will examine what they observe as important in the relationship between humans and their environment as yet another way of interpreting literary landscape. As we explore the ways women authors, such as Jane Austen, create heroines and their response to landscape, we will also note ways that male authors create a different response to the landscape by their heroines. I have the same interest in "socially constructed" landscape, landscape that "reflects human values and ideologies of the resident and viewer" (Ringer 7) as do aesthetic geographers such as George Hughes. Hughes uses a "concept of liminality to describe the 'betwixt and between' moments when people are disposed to feel liberated from the norms of their society" (Ringer 22). A limen—or threshold—is the demarcation between one landscape and another. The seashore, possibly at Lyme Regis, exemplifies the best example of a liminal space, one with fluid boundaries. Austen uses such places to provide freedom of movement for heroines.

Cresswell discusses one powerful ideological strategy: to naturalize a place, to cover up the social and historical aspects to provide what the author wants in landscape and call it "only natural." We will examine this strategy as well and how it provides a way of looking at what Jane Austen does with her landscape and her frequent use of the expression "only natural." Cresswell has discussed women transgressing and transforming space. Jane Austen certainly provides examples of heroines both transgressing and transforming space. If space is used to control people and things, a novelist such as Jane Austen will certainly try to arrange her "space" accordingly.

Definitions of the term "landscape" vary. Historian Denis Cosgrove describes it this way:

> Landscape ... is an ideological concept. It represents a way in which certain classes of people have signified themselves and their world through their imagined relationship with nature, and through which they have underlined and communicated their own social role and that of others with respect to external nature. (15)

This definition includes not only how certain classes of people see the world but also how gender affects the way landscape is seen. The gaze upon the landscape means something quite different for a woman—author or heroine—than it does for a man. When an eighteenth-century male with a background in the gentry gazes on the landscape, he frames it in a way that objectifies it and indicates its potential for control. When a woman gazes, she is imagining where she fits inside the landscape and how she can position herself to be helped by it.

One of the most influential feminist writers on geography—space—is Gillian Rose. In *Feminism and Geography*, Rose maintains that "spaces are felt as part of patriarchal power" (146). She goes on to assert that, because men have done the controlling of space, women find it necessary to resist the choices of confinement or exclusion, in a way, "both being prisoner and exile, both within and without" (159). Even earlier in the feminist critique of environmental positioning, we can go to Sherry Ortner's work examining the associations of women with nature and men with culture, particularly in Western civilization. Although I use the oppositional and seemingly essential terms of inside/outside and nature/culture, they remain fluid. (As Rose has shown us, one can be both confined and excluded, prisoner and exile.) The protagonists in novels may be associated with nature/culture, outsider/insider, and masculine/feminine, or they may find themselves associated with qualities on either side. I am not asserting that all males act one way and females another, whether characters or novelists; however, with men in economic control of land and society in late eighteenth- and early nineteenth-century Britain, women had to find a way to adapt, survive, and succeed creatively within that framework. They could join the men in their pursuits, or, if they had their own agenda regarding position in the landscape, they could openly transgress on male territory, or they could quietly transform the scene. Deborah Kaplan in *Jane Austen among Women* uses the term "dual cultural responses." Kaplan explains that women's culture differs from the culture of the gentry at that time and that Austen, being part of both cultures, expressed a cultural duality. Kaplan finds in Austen's works "covert or oblique expressions of Austen's subversive perspectives." But Kaplan also sees that Austen's novels "champion the gentry's culture" (13). "Dual responses" (similar to the ability to understand and use two dialects) express the sometimes conflicting ways in which Austen's heroines view their landscapes.

Although artists have long regarded landscape as an important means of expression, geographers have only recently begun to focus specifically upon landscape and its meanings. Landscape, according to Rose, "is a central term in geographical studies because it refers to one of the discipline's most enduring interests: the relation between Nature and Culture" ("Looking at Landscape" 342). In *Iconography of Landscape*, Cosgrove and Daniels call landscape "a cultural image, a pictorial way of representing, structuring or symbolising surroundings" (1). In *The Idea of Landscape*, Denis Cosgrove explores the cultural and historical influences on landscape and how it is perceived. As an historical geographer, Cosgrove attributes the transition to capitalism during the period of about 1400-1900 as the time when the idea of landscape began to evolve. During this period, landscape "came to denote the artistic and literary representation of the visible world, the scenery (literally that which is *seen*)" (*Idea* 9). Another, and no longer conflicting definition, for landscape is the more scientific "integration of natural and human phenomena which can be empirically verified and analysed by the methods of scientific enquiry over a delimited portion of the earth's surface" (*Idea* 9).

As I look at Jane Austen's work, my own definition of "landscape," while heavily influenced by Appleton, Cosgrove, Cresswell, Rose, and others, remains quite broad: it includes how the natural outdoor setting is perceived, including elements of that setting which might occasionally move indoors. So landscape begins as a recognition of the natural world around us having value, both socially and financially but moving from that definition, which relates best to cultural geography, to one which is more the interpretation of the natural setting by an artist, and, in the case of Jane Austen, a novelist. As we more closely focus our definition of landscape, we will see it from the perspective of a female novelist from the minor gentry, certainly a tenuous position financially, in early nineteenth-century southern England. As we examine Jane Austen's work from her early writing to the efforts of the last months of her life, we will focus particularly on how the heroines use the natural places to find for themselves protective shields and sources of encouragement—places to hide and places to seek a fulfilling existence.

The Picturesque

> "An object is said to be picturesque in proportion as it would have a good effect in a picture ... it is applied solely to the works of nature."
> —Joshua Reynolds (qtd from Hipple 199)

Examining Jane Austen's landscape involves understanding the picturesque, what it meant to Austen, and how her own landscapes both satirize and exemplify the picturesque. Although many critics have written about Austen in a variety of ways, only a few have dealt with her landscapes, in particular, her use of the picturesque. The picturesque is the kind of landscape Reverend William Gilpin suggests should be framed, either as a painting or a Claude glass view from a specific site by a traveler; he writes that the observers should "examine scenery of nature by the rules of painting" (*Three Essays of Picturesque Beauty* 42). Edmund Burke, in his *Philosophical Enquiry into the Origin of our Ideas of the Sublime and Beautiful* (1757), influenced later landscape aestheticians from Gilpin to Uvedale Price, Richard Payne Knight, and finally Humphry Repton, landscape improver. Each has a somewhat different notion of what "picturesque" means, but they all find that it lies somewhere between the sublime and beautiful, giving the viewer a scene which is neither totally awesome nor totally beautiful, in other words, an English landscape. All of them would probably have agreed that the picturesque landscape has a roughness or irregularity in the topography, possibly a small cottage, or a ruin in the scene, certainly clumps of foliage, neither entirely beautiful (associated with femininity) nor sublime (associated with masculinity).

However, Repton, the only practicing landscape gardener of the group, went further than simply framing the scene. He actively added and removed features to enhance his own notion of the picturesque. Malcolm Andrews, in *The Search for the Picturesque*, finds that picturesque scenery becomes a kind of commodity: the picturesque artist "'appropriates' natural scenery and processes it into a commodity ... converts Nature's unmanageable bounty into a frameable possession" (81). Perspective was extremely important, and the lowest possible viewpoint was usually suggested. Art began to shift from reason to imagination, i.e. a "ruin" evolves from being a lesson in mutability to becoming a structure with melancholy associations. One traveled with pictures as a guide to the actual scenery in the 1790s, and the picturesque painting was framed with stage designs. Gilpin found foregrounds essential to landscape in a way that distances were not. When a picturesque traveler viewed the landscape with his Claude glass, he or she was able to frame it and see it reflected back with some of the details lost.

Two of the few scholars who focus on Austen's landscape are Mavis Batey and Philippa Tristram. Batey, in *Jane Austen and the English Landscape*, presents an excellent analysis of Austen's landscapes from an historical perspective. In *Living Space in Fact and Fiction*, Philippa Tristram does a remarkable job of discussing Austen's ambivalence to improvement. Although Tristram does not spend much time on landscape alone, she does deal with cottages. Cottages, during the Regency period, refer to many kinds of dwellings, confusing the reader about the social prominence of the owner. According to Tristram, Austen's main problem with middle-class cottages lay in the dishonesty with which they are frequently represented. For instance, when Robert Ferrars claims to be "excessively fond of a cottage" (255), Austen satirizes the false modesty his mention of what had once been considered a dwelling of the poor and now has evolved into a lavish cottage ornée.

Some other critics who have dealt primarily with Jane Austen and the picturesque are Alistair Duckworth (*The Improvement of the Estate*), Roger Sales (*Writers and Place in England* and *Jane Austen and Regency England*), and, more recently, Jill Heydt-Stevenson ("Liberty, Connection, and Tyranny: The Novels of Jane Austen and the Aesthetic Movement of the Picturesque"). Alistair Duckworth's *The Improvement of the Estate* remains an influential work on Jane Austen and landscape. Published in 1971, Duckworth's book argues that Austen "affirms society, ideally considered as a structure of values that are ultimately founded in religious principle, at the same time as she distinguishes it from its frequently corrupted form" (28). Duckworth's view, along with that of Marilyn Butler (*Jane*

Austen and the War of Ideas), is generally regarded as conservative—emphasizing Austen's admiration for a Burkean notion of building on the embodiment and wisdom of past generations. Duckworth's argument focuses upon how Austen uses the great country houses of her novels to show where the Burkean ideas went astray and to examine what Austen believes to be the place of the individual in an ideal community based upon religion and morality. Many passages in Austen's novels convince us that she certainly seems to be showing the reader where society has become corrupted, but in 1971, Duckworth's scope did not include the perspective of women specifically.

In His "Preface to the Paperback Edition," published in 1994, Duckworth reviews some of the feminist criticism that was published during the intervening twenty-three years. He concedes that Margaret Kirkham and Claudia Johnson have made him more aware of Austen's focus on women's issues as they describe "an author who delighted in the energy, wit, and moral independence of women and who could be acerbically critical of masculine coercion, authoritarianism, and complacency" (ix). Yet he argues that Johnson ignores Austen's use of estate metaphors which imply "a Burkean defense of a culture heritage" (x). He does not share her belief that Austen and Mary Wollstonecraft had much in common. Austen "sought accommodation for her ideals within existing, albeit imperfect, social structures; Wollstonecraft did not," and Austen, according to Duckworth, "shows no sign of promoting alternative roles for women" (x), as does Wollstonecraft.

While I attempt to show in this book a landscape with the Burkean underpinnings which Duckworth so aptly attributes to the ideal estate, I also intend to move into the natural landscape, using geography and feminism as two different lenses with which to approach Austen's fiction. One can never forget that Jane Austen is writing from a woman's point of view, aware of women's issues, problems, and treatment in the society of her time. Although her novels reflect the thinking of prominent men such as Edmund Burke and Samuel Johnson, she somehow must find ways for herself and other women to exert power in society. I argue that Austen illustrates ways of achieving a sense of power by her placement of women in the natural landscape, not necessarily focusing on the great estates alone. I agree with Duckworth that Austen is neither "radical" nor "progressive" (xi-xii), yet her heroines model their own ways of circumventing the existing patriarchal culture as they use the landscape to advance their goals. Austen could imagine heroines creating a free space within existing society and transforming it, while clearly admiring what Burke felt English society ought to do: to preserve and to adapt existing institutions.

Roger Sales in his chapter on Jane Austen in *Writers and Place in England* writes: "One marvel of her fiction is the way her precision is employed; Austen can take bits and pieces of geography and landscape and transform them into social tone and moral suggestion in a sentence or two" (35). However, he argues that Austen moves from an idea of place, one that "floats unattached in the novel" (39) toward an "embodiment" of place, which first appears at Pemberley, as Austen frees herself from the landscapes of southern England with which she is almost too familiar (41). Sales believes that with the scene at Pemberley, Austen disassociates herself from the landscapes which she knew first, and her imaginative sense of space takes over, creating more detailed and unique landscapes that become more integral to the novels. Generally speaking, Sales is correct: Landscapes in *Northanger Abbey* and *Sense and Sensibility* do not compare with that famous scene at Pemberley, but both the juvenilia and the earlier works highlight how important scenes of her personal landscape were to Austen.

Jill Heydt-Stevenson discusses the connections between the picturesque and feminism in a way that none of her predecessors had. In her article, she differentiates between the picturesque aesthetic and landscape improvement. Improvement, she claims, can be "despotic," particularly for women. She uses Fanny Price as an example of a female protagonist who is unnaturally forced into an "improved" place by Sir Thomas and Mrs. Norris. Although Austen has been frequently described as a conservative Tory, her concept of the aesthetic picturesque, which values organic growth, national pride and preservation, also "leads to a liberal and feminist attitude toward women, for in identifying her heroines with the landscape of picturesque aesthetics, she associates them with freedom, playfulness, introspection, and connection to others, to their landscape and to their nation" (Heydt-Stevenson 274). Heydt-Stevenson's placement of Austen in line with the ideas of organic growth and national pride, coupled with the identification of her heroines with picturesque landscapes, comes closest to my way of thinking. I agree with Heydt-Stevenson's argument that Austen found a way of championing women through her use of picturesque landscape aesthetics, but I want to push beyond what Heydt-Stevenson has argued, looking at Austen's picturesque landscape through the lenses of aesthetic geographers as well.

I am arguing that women can create private spaces within the landscape that offer them the power of knowledge gained through their own silent, and sometimes invisible, observation. These prospects from which to see and hidden refuges from which to avoid notice exist in all six of Jane Austen's novels, as well as in her juvenilia and her final, unfinished novel, *Sanditon*. The landscapes of England in Austen's novels extend the range of reflection and activity of her female protagonists. Austen's representation of the landscape develops from open satire of the late eighteenth-century landscapes of sensibility in her youthful pieces to an expanded exploration of where the female protagonists find themselves in the cultural and economic landscapes of England.

To illustrate that women writers have found that landscape poses a significant problem for their female protagonists, we need only look to the novels of Fanny Burney and Ann Radcliffe. Their plots involving female protagonists reveal the dangers of a male-dominated landscape but do not find any clear ways for their heroines to handle these problems alone. Jane Austen admired these novelists and was only too familiar with their landscapes, but she responded differently, even in her youthful efforts at describing landscape. In her juvenilia, Austen drew upon scenes from her novel-reading experiences and exaggerated them as she illustrated the problems of a man coming to town and casually appropriating the landscape and the landowner's daughter for himself. Yet other landscapes in her early writing were used openly, and to great effect, by girls. All of these landscapes, as her more mature ones, existed as palimpsests of her memories of reading other landscapes by Gilpin and earlier novelists.

Although Austen's teenaged writing displays the most intense satire of characters interacting with landscape, her six novels portray women with differing needs for prospects and refuges, based upon their age and social status. All of Austen's female protagonists encounter what Appleton refers to as "landscapes of exposure"; however, the oldest and most mature heroine, Anne Elliot, deals with exposure much better than does the more impulsive, less mature, Marianne Dashwood. In fact, the earlier heroines, Catherine Morland, Marianne Dashwood, and Elizabeth Bennet find their confidence increasing as they learn from such landscapes of exposure. They are initially vulnerable and only aware of landscape from second-hand knowledge until they actually find themselves struggling with learning what their identity within the landscape *is*.

Edge-of-the-wood experiences form another important way for Austen's heroines to understand and control where they are in the landscape. These situations involve what Appleton describes as "zones of safety." They may be boundary walks, such as the one from which Elizabeth Bennett learns so much, or they may be places near park palings, good places to hide and to seek, experienced by Fanny Price and Charlotte Heywood. The concept of liminality provides significant situations for the heroines to learn what is beneficial to them—moments such as hiding in the hedgerow or encountering the sea. All these landscapes provide ways for women to control their lives. In these places, women find ways to both transgress and transform the landscape.

Basically what Austen would have all her heroines find in the landscape is a real notion of who they are—of self. Fanny Price internalizes the landscape of Mansfield Park; Emma learns what is really "natural" in Highbury and its environs. Anne Elliot finds her "self" by leaving home and eventually looks forward to moving beyond the liminal seashore and going to sea. In contrast, Walter Scott's heroine, Jeanie Deans of *Heart of Midlothian*, provides an example of how a male author's heroine does not mediate a position in favor of self as a free woman but basically exemplifies Scott's own moral and historical position.

In any case, Austen's heroines mediate a position which allows them greater awareness of who they are and what they can be. They move between a landscape conceived by the male-dominated culture of the time while recognizing a landscape which provides safety and camouflage for them. Significantly, the female protagonists in Austen's fiction find ways of combining emotional, biological, and artistic strategies to find what, for them, are the "best" places. Jane Austen maps out her views on landscape as early as her juvenile writings and, what she left the world in her last unfinished work, *Sanditon*, is a landscape rich in the possibilities for showing us a heroine who will deal with landscape as a primary agent of change in the novel itself.

The next chapter, "The Potential of Death by Landscape," provides some context for examining the landscape of Jane Austen. In it, the reader moves from a study of Margaret Atwood's short story, "Death by Landscape," and its implications for heroines and how they perceive their landscape, to an examination of the relationship between the heroines of Fanny Burney and Ann Radcliffe and their landscapes. Atwood's story provides a clear example of the effect of landscape on women even today and illustrates the ways women deal with it, even when they have some economic power, something few eighteenth-century heroines had. Appleton's prospect/refuge theory of aesthetic geography is explained more fully, so that the reader can use it as a reference for answering the following question: What is a "safe" place for a woman (or anyone for that matter) and how can it be recognized aesthetically in literature? As we examine how the male prospect viewers of the eighteenth century observed landscape, we begin to understand the problem for women in finding a "zone of compromise," a way of being *in* the landscape without being *part* of it. Like Lois from Atwood's twentieth-century short story, as soon as these women "step off the path," they lose their safe place as well as their prospect. Both Burney and Radcliffe tell the story of the landscape but have none of the confidence of the male landscape spectators or any illusions concerning their control of it. Their heroines (like Lois) are not satisfied to be *in* or *out* of the landscape, neither the passive Lucy of Wordsworthian fame nor the spectator, owning the scene. Ultimate control of the landscape and the potential danger of a male presence there, trying to objectify women, converting them to property, are prominent themes and ones that persist into the present day. The readings of *Evelina* and *The Mysteries of Udolpho* act as guides for observing the heroines in the landscape of Jane Austen.

Following our study of Jane Austen's predecessors, Chapter Three, "Four White Cows Disposed at Equal Distances—or—Steel Traps to Bowers in Austen's Short Fiction" examines her own youthful efforts at viewing the landscape. As a precocious adolescent, Jane Austen recognized, from her considerable experience in reading (and somewhat less in society), that men controlled the landscape. Male "improvers" seeded the grounds with steel traps and erected park palings. Girls were nymphs or sad suicidals, experiencing "death by landscape." This chapter looks at the landscape of her early writing and examines the way Jane Austen portrays her characters in their landscape. "Evelyn" reveals a man who easily appropriates a stereotypical eighteenth-century aesthetic landscape. This short fictional piece contrasts with "Catharine,—Or The Bower," which shows just how an Austen heroine can construct her own landscape and use it as a means of both transforming and transgressing space. The Bower is, in fact, the perfect aesthetic landscape, providing a place to hide, and yet a place to seek, a liminal space where a girl gets the chance to stand at the threshold of freedom from societal restraints and yet retreat to her childhood home. Austen's exuberant adolescent writing really does provide the key to her more mature works; in fact, it may be the very "lens" through which to read everything else she wrote subsequently. Her landscapes here show a clear notion of male prospect viewing, all the while making light of that same notion and suggesting a clear alternative in the shape of a female-friendly bower which a girl can construct for herself.

In Chapter Four, "Heroines-in-Training: The First Three," we move on to *Northanger Abbey*, *Sense and Sensibility*, and *Pride and Prejudice*, where the heroines find themselves in exposed landscapes. They discover that learning is the way of successfully surviving, and asserting that knowledge over the landscape transforms them from victims to the kind of women they want to be from the start— women who understand themselves and those around them in ways that enhance all their lives. So the act of experiencing the landscape is a double one, helping the heroine—or heroine-in-training—to interpret the world and to know her own "self," transforming both world and self.

Chapter Five, "Enclaves of Civility amidst Clamorous Impertinence," deals with heroines who move from zones of safety to landscapes of exposure—exposure not so much to their physical safety but more to their true sense of self. Using

Appleton's aesthetic geographical perspective, we see how the "right" landscape provides a way for each heroine to control her own destiny as well as stare down the prospect of finding herself in a landscape of social exposure, with only her "self" to count on. As we examine the landscape of *Mansfield Park*, we look more closely at Fanny's real place: the landscape both "cures" her and she "cures" the landscape. As we read in *Emma* about scenes that are "only natural," we learn that "natural" can have a number of different meanings, all of which the heroine needs to grasp in order to discover who she really is. But in either case—Fanny's or Emma's—the heroine leaves her "home"—be it Mansfield or Hartfield—only to return to it with a deeper sense that her true influence is there.

In Chapter Six, "The Geography of *Persuasion*," we see how Austen pushes beyond the landscape she has previously used as a place for her heroines to achieve happiness. Although another female contemporary of Jane Austen, Hannah More, perceives woman's place as being in her own little garden, Anne Elliot is forced to contemplate what it is like to have "a beloved home made over to others." The garden does not belong to her anymore, and she can only survey these former "home scenes" with the permission of the new residents. In a very real way, the heroine has lost her heritage, unlike Fanny, who reclaims the proper heritage for everyone. Anne finds her *self* in a sensitive connection with her landscape—a landscape that is more than her ancestral home at Kellynch, a landscape through which she can read her deepest feelings in the present and understand her past. This is a landscape containing a deep cultural impression and possibly something that goes beyond culture—an evolutionary landscape, one where a person's response to its beauty is rooted deeply in its functionality and its survival possibilities. Using *The Heart of Midlothian*, we can compare how Austen's contemporary and admirer Sir Walter Scott places his heroine, Jeannie Deans, in the landscape. Finally, we see that Austen's way of dealing with landscape does not "fit" with either Scott's or More's, but she gives a new sense of freedom in the environment to her heroines.

Chapter Seven, "*Sanditon*: Half Topography, Half Romance," really does illustrate Annie Proulx's notion that "landscapes rise from the page, to appear in the camera lens of the reader's mind." E. M. Forster describes the novel fragment *Sanditon* as having "a double-flavoured taste—half topography, half romance." Brian Southam, in a discussion of *Sanditon*, writes: "Ultimately, in *Sanditon*, the setting becomes an agent in the story." We can ask a number of questions of this last and incomplete novel of Jane Austen. Is the place what we, the readers, think it is? Or—can a place be what we wish it to be? Does the notion of a seaside resort represent the improver's dream or does it become that "double-flavoured" thing—half-topography, half-romance? Or—maybe both? Since this novel remained incomplete, my study only speculates about the answers to these questions.

The key to our understanding of a resort like Sanditon, the watering place, and Sanditon House, the old estate, as well as Willingden, Brinshore, and the geography of the southeast coast of England, may lie with Charlotte Heywood. She has the ability to "transgress" and potentially "transform" the landscape, as she observes more and forms new judgments, questioning the naturalness of the old, low-lying places and the new "sparkling views" of the sea. Although others have attempted to complete this fragment, what Charlotte Heywood finally accomplishes will never truly be known.

My study ends with a brief retrospective on early critical responses to Austen's novelistic landscapes, Charlotte Brontë's reactions to Austen's purportedly "prim," manicured landscapes, and finally, directions women writers today are following in their regard to landscape.

***

From her early writing to the fragmentary work of her last months, Jane Austen's fiction is deeply connected to landscape. In the following chapters, I ask the reader to take an aesthetic geographical lens—a Claude glass, if you will—and view her landscape through it. I believe Jane Austen positions her heroines to subvert a male-dominated landscape in ways that allow them to stand at a threshold—a zone of safety—between prospect and refuge. I have focused particularly on the early writing and *Sanditon*, devoting an entire chapter to each, because they have been given less attention in the past than the more popular novels and also because they demonstrate Austen's attention to landscape and its particular connection with the female characters at both the beginning and end of her writing career. In her last two works, *Persuasion* and *Sanditon*, the prospect is opening even wider as the sea becomes the focal point of future growth for these women. However, throughout all of her works, Jane Austen finds opportunities for women to use landscape as a way to advance successfully into their futures.

Chapter 2

The Potential of Death by Landscape

Habitat theory. The theory that aesthetic satisfaction experienced in the contemplation of landscape stems from the spontaneous perception of landscape features which, in their shapes, colours, spatial arrangements and other visible attributes, act as sign-stimuli indicative of environmental conditions favourable for survival, whether they are really favourable or not.

(Appleton 269)

"In every perception of nature there is actually present the whole of society."
—Theodor Adorno (Eisenman 141)

Margaret Atwood's short story, "Death by Landscape" (1991), depicts a wilderness, at once threatening, perplexing, yet exhilarating for the women caught up in it. As teenagers at summer camp, Lois and Lucy are on a canoe trip when Lucy "stepped sideways and disappeared from time" (151). Lois spends the rest of her life searching for a way to deal with this terrifying landscape, all the while carrying her friend's existence around with her—along with almost overwhelming guilt concerning her part in Lucy's disappearance.[1] As an older adult, Lois feels compelled to collect landscape paintings. Her male friends, who see landscape as "commodity," admire her as a shrewd art investor; however, her reason for collecting the paintings is to search for her lost friend in the landscape. "Looking at them fills her with a wordless unease. Despite the fact that there are no people

---

[1] The choice of the name "Lucy" may reflect the idea of woman and landscape as united, as in Wordsworth's Lucy poems where Lucy dies and becomes a part of the landscape. "Three Years She Grew" (1800) particularly comes to mind:
>Three years she grew in sun and shower,
>Then Nature said, "A lovelier flower
>On earth was never sown;
>This Child I to myself will take;
>She shall be mine, and I will make
>A Lady of my own." (ll. 1-6)

>Thus Nature spake—the work was done—
>How soon my Lucy's race was run!
>She died, and left to me
>This heath, this calm, and quiet scene;
>The memory of what has been,
>And never more will be. (ll. 37-42)

In "Naturalizing Gender: Woman's Place in Wordsworth's Ideological Landscape" (*English Literary History* vol. 53 1986), Marlon Ross writes of the Lucy poems, "Lucy's voice is nonexistent in the poem and just at the point at which she may be allowed to speak, she is silenced with death" (397).

in them or even animals, it's as if there is something, or someone, looking back out" (129).

Atwood's narrative compresses many of the hopes and fears of earlier women writers and the relationship their heroines have with their landscape into one short story. Atwood portrays Lois as a woman who "was living not one life but two: her own and another shadowy life that hovered around her and would not let itself be realized" (151). Lois, as other heroines in literature, spends much of her life trying to fit into a landscape where neither refuge nor prospect seems to exist—where there is no place to hide or to seek.

Lois's attempts to find a way to mediate her existence in a landscape that seems antithetical to women, one that seems to want to absorb them and deny their individuality, remain unsuccessful. Lois succeeds in recognizing that her life has been an unconscious struggle with the landscape and that studying her landscape paintings at least helps her to revise the story of Lucy, and, as she realizes at the very end of the story, "to keep Lucy entirely alive"(153). We can trace this recognition of the mediation between female subject and her landscape back to the eighteenth-century novels by women. It is a difficult mediation indeed, fraught with violent action and a search for a zone of safety and compromise from which the heroine might gain some control or at least some understanding of her existence.[2]

The description of Lois's landscape paintings (all by men) in Atwood's story closely resembles the themes from earlier British novels:

> And these paintings are not landscape paintings. Because there aren't any landscapes up there, not in the old, tidy European sense, with a gentle hill, a curving river, a cottage, a mountain in the background, a golden evening sky. Instead there's a tangle, a receding maze, in which you can become lost almost as soon as you step off the path. There are no backgrounds in any of these paintings, no vistas; only a great deal of foreground that goes back and back, endlessly, involving you in its twists and turns of tree and branch and rock. No matter how far back in you go, there will be more. And the trees themselves are hardly trees; they are currents of energy, charged with violent colour. (152)

The Canadian landscape paintings do not represent the contained, neat eighteenth-century European picturesque scenes, but the sensations that Lois experiences resemble those of Fanny Burney and Ann Radcliffe's heroines from the late eighteenth century. Although my intent is not to compare twentieth-century writers with those of the eighteenth century at any length, I think it is significant to note that Atwood and Austen have some common threads in their fictional work. They both have female protagonists attempting to reconcile themselves to male-dominated landscapes and to find a way to come to terms with that landscape, not allowing it to dominate them. The endings of "Death by Landscape" and Jane Austen's novels illustrate women who have found a new sense of self that co-exists with the

---

[2] Chapter 4 of *Marxism and Literature* by Raymond Williams provides a helpful discussion of the old idea of reflection, which is challenged by the term mediation, a more active process, an "act of intercession." In one sense Williams describes mediation as "reconciliation, or interpretation between adversaries or strangers" (97), although in a neutral sense it may be considered "interaction by separate forces." Still mediation remains a "term to describe the process of relationship between 'society' and 'art'" (98).

landscape. These heroines refuse to become just an attractive part of the scene; they use the landscape to their advantage.

Something in the controlled eighteenth-century male-spectator's view of the landscape persistently unravels for women and does not "suit" them. Their perception of the landscape deviates from Pope's point of view in "Windsor Forest," where men clearly control the scene. Women can tell the story of the landscape but have no illusions about who controls it. As soon as these women "step off the path," they lose their safe place and their prospect. Lois handles this sense of disorientation in the landscape by a realization of its "currents of energy, charged with violent colour" and by containing that energy in the frame of a picture/story. If she cannot force any real and final closure on such a bounded work, at least she can keep the "Lucy" side of herself from becoming totally forgotten and absorbed within an otherwise meaningless and chaotic landscape. "She looks at the paintings, she looks into them. Every one of them is a picture of Lucy" (152).

Whether during the eighteenth century or the twenty-first, the relationship between the author's gender and the way the heroine interacts with her landscape reveals something of the gender perceptions and stereotypes of the time and the ways in which women writers have circumvented these. (Many of these stereotypes have persisted through the ages.) Of the many ways a reader can locate the heroine in the landscape, one approach reveals the landscape as a layering of past and present for the viewer—a palimpsest. The palimpsest of the previous landscape in any narrative consists of many physical, cultural, and sociological strata, imperfectly revealed under the most recent landscape. So landscape, as has been discussed earlier, consists of many things, all in combination to be read by the protagonist, and if read astutely, the female protagonist can negotiate her way to the "safest" parts of it, avoiding danger and finding refuge.

As we consider this mediation of heroine and landscape, we may focus upon ways in which men and women perceive their landscapes differently because of cultural orientations and aesthetic geography, indicating that landscape's beauty and interest reflect how individuals perceive a habitat as a good place to survive. While our major thrust remains the position of female characters, particularly the heroines, in Jane Austen's landscape, we might understand her interest in landscape viewing better in light of her predecessors, Fanny Burney and Anne Radcliffe, novelists familiar to both Austen and Atwood.

What about Lois's (and Lucy's) forebears, Burney's Evelina and Radcliffe's Emily? Margaret Atwood may well have felt the influence of these women writers and the interaction of their heroines with the landscape, as well as their heroines' abilities to frame their own landscapes, providing a way for them to hide and seek—to survive with dignity. Two late eighteenth-century novels written by women, *Evelina* (1778) by Fanny Burney and *The Mysteries of Udolpho* (1794) by Ann Radcliffe, show heroines (like Lois) who are neither satisfied to be *in* or *out* of the landscape.

As we look at these two novels, we recognize how women novelists situate their heroines in the landscape. We will examine the ways in which the landscape remains a danger to the heroines, who fear losing themselves to masculine dominance, a prominent theme in these late eighteenth-century novels and one which persists throughout the nineteenth century. The readings of these novels work as guides for observing the heroines in the landscape of Jane Austen.

The theme of the heroine trapped between two positions, the one a static, passive fusion with landscape and the other a nascent attempt to control it herself, is revealed in Burney's and Radcliffe's works. Being trapped in a "no-woman's land" remains a problem for heroines in many of the works we will look at from Austen's early juvenile piece, "Jack and Alice," to her last effort, *Sanditon*. However, Burney and Radcliffe treat the problem quite differently than does Austen.

To understand the positioning of any viewer of the landscape, we must remember eighteenth-century historical/aesthetic changes in awareness of landscape perception. Burney's use of conventional landscape perception, as described by art historians and critics, begins to reveal the vulnerability of women in the landscape. As we continue to focus upon the position of the heroine, we must also remember Jay Appleton's concept of safety involving a "zone of compromise"—a good place for the heroine to hide and to seek. The scenes from *Evelina* reveal a heroine caught in a male-controlled landscape where no zone of compromise exists. Because Evelina has no refuge (where a woman can be one with landscape) or prospect (where a woman can control landscape), she is subject to the full force of male violence present in that landscape. Later women writers, such as Jane Austen, find ways for their heroines to mediate a place in the landscape, but in Evelina, Burney only projects the frightened helplessness of her heroine.

Besides the physical place of the heroine, landscape as a layering of past landscapes—narratological palimpsests—becomes an important factor in viewing the scene, both for the heroine and for the reader. The past experience—both physical and intellectual—of the heroine contributes to her regard of the landscape. Narratologist Gerard Genette has emphasized the importance of the landscape viewer's background in perceiving a present landscape. What layers of past landscapes—baggage—are brought along by both the heroine and the author? These layers exist due to both the gender experiences of the heroine and those of the novelist writing about her. Even the spatial metaphor of "separate spheres" for men and women in the nineteenth century suggests that each gender draws upon different materials out of which to construct a landscape.

Twentieth-century (and early twenty-first century) psychologists, geographers, and feminist literary critics suggest that women bring these culturally influenced gender experiences to their interactions with landscape even today. In *The Mysteries of Udolpho*, Radcliffe brings into her heroine's palimpsest of the landscape, the whole tradition of the eighteenth-century male landscape spectator, along with nascent questioning of the pride in control of landscape exemplified by male aestheticians. The previous eighteenth-century glorification of a landscape that represents Gothic liberty and Roman authority Radcliffe turns into an unframed (therefore uncontrollable) terrifying landscape with neither freedom nor safety for the heroine. Burney and Radcliffe recognize that women have a very tenuous existence in a landscape with which they both want to harmonize and yet control. Their heroines are aware of their vulnerable positions in the landscape, but it remains for later women novelists to find ways for their heroines to mediate a more comfortable place there.

Politically, Burney and Radcliffe have few similarities, yet their landscapes use the same old male conventions of landscape description—with a twist. The landscapes sometimes go out of control, moving into what might seem to be a shockingly unfeminine area of violence—one which later heroines (such as Lois) increasingly recognize, although they still cannot seem to avoid it. The heroines in these novels are not satisfied to be an unquestioning part of the landscape, yet they never feel satisfactorily in control of it. Far from appropriating the landscape as a commodity or managing the malleable mass of nature to the desired shape attempted by earlier male landscape viewers, these women writers, and their heroines, face the difficulties of controlling the landscape, all the while recognizing that their male critics harbor very clear ideas of the limitations of "authoresses"— either of books or of their own fate.

"I don't know what the devil a woman lives for after thirty; she is only in other folks' way," declares the obnoxious middle-class suitor of Evelina. Margaret Anne Doody describes *Evelina* as a novel where Evelina's trials growing up "reflect the errors in her society rather than herself" (*Frances Burney* 46). As her later novels, *Evelina*, Burney's first novel, exhibits aggression against women (who are many times "missing" last names) and the anxiety which these women experience. Most men, regardless of class, appear as threats; in fact, Doody calls *Evelina* "antimasculinist satire" (65). Like Burney's later novel *Camilla*, *Evelina* explains "conduct manual" behavior for women, but, as Doody comments concerning the later novel, under the surface, it is a critique of male behavior and what men try to force women to learn. Landscape, then, is not the only area where Burney seems to express mixed feelings, using the conventional landscape aesthetic as well as deviating from it. As another critic notes, Burney "represents a paradox of the times—a schizophrenic ability to see the gross exaggeration of feeling in sentimental rhetoric and yet to deal in it" (Murray 45). Evelina recognizes the overly sentimental address of a would-be lover and rejects it. Yet the novel remains full of examples of sentimental rhetoric that Burney must perceive as the "appropriate" kind.

Conventionally sentimental or not, the landscape intrigues the reader. The landscape of *Evelina* consists of paths (literal and figurative)—paths from which women deviate only at their physical peril (as do Atwood's Lucy and Lois). Yet, Fanny Burney is not the only female writer of her time to use women and paths together. Noted evangelist and writer, Hannah More, uses the same path image to show how a woman racing with a man "in the career of genius" is more likely than the man to become distracted by beauty at the side of the road, losing the race (*Strictures* 27). In More's imaginary race, upon losing, the woman must marry the winner. The insecurity of the early women novelists in their landscape contrasts rather sharply with their masculine contemporaries. In many of the landscape paintings and poems of the eighteenth century, the point of view is generally that of a controlling prospect-viewer who does not confine himself to a narrow path but enjoys a broad overview of the scene.

Burney begins her novel using the conventional controlling devices of the scenes used by the male artists before her. She was always fascinated with theater (and wrote several plays, a few of which enjoyed some popularity at the time), and a stage-like effect exists in many of her novels. The broadly played character of Mme. Duval resembles the transvestite "larger than life" stage dame. Doody calls *Evelina* "sustained emphatic and expressionistic farce" (*Frances Burney* 48). The early scenes of the novel, set in ballrooms (and even the theater itself) as well as the later scenes in the pump room, suggest the control of a proscenium framing the setting of the novel.[3]

But the instability and vulnerability that Evelina experiences in the natural settings suggest concerns of the author about position in the landscape. "We regard all landscapes as symbolic, as expressions of cultural values, social behavior, and individual actions worked upon particular localities over a span of time," writes D. W. Meinig. Adding to Meinig's interpretation of landscape, I suggest that gender also helps to construct the landscape (if we agree that gender is a social and cultural construct). The landscape of "home" is examined by David Sopher who states that "home has no meaning apart from the journey which takes one outside home" (Meinig 133) and home has to do with people and memories. Not only in Burney's and Radcliffe's novels is the theme of home crucial, but also in *Mansfield Park*, *Emma*, and *Persuasion*, the heroines find themselves trapped in boundary areas between old familiar homes and new unknown ones. The same concern for the location of home exists in the male-authored novels, such as *The Heart of Midlothian* by Jane Austen's contemporary, Sir Walter Scott, but male authors have a different relationship to their heroines than do the female authors; it is more historical and nationalistic in nature. What eventually becomes "home" for these women in female-authored novels involves not only emotional connections but viable means of physical support as well.

Not all of Burney's landscapes have stage-like features, and her heroine becomes deeply confused in landscapes away from home. Some landscapes place Evelina on paths that are dark, threatening, and obscure. A "zone of compromise"—a narrow area with access to refuge and prospect for the heroine—becomes dangerously constricted and, at times, nonexistent. Part of the danger to women in these scenes emanates from a kind of out-of-control aggression—savage jokes on the part of supposedly civil men such as Captain Mirvan and his companions as they roam around the landscape threatening women.

Doody mentions the practical jokers who go beyond the civil limits, one outstanding example of this excess being the scene that includes the old women's footrace (another race that no woman can really "win"). Certainly no zone of compromise exists for the two infirm women who are forced to compete in a race where the bored lords place bets on who will win. When Evelina tries to rescue one of the women who has fallen with a great deal of force on the gravel path, one of the lords cries, "'No foul play!" (294). At last one woman falls and "was too much hurt to move, and declared her utter inability to make another attempt. Mr. Coverley was quite brutal: he swore at her with unmanly rage, and seemed scarce able to refrain even from striking her" (294). Evelina's description of the dangerous path of two women makes the horror of exposed landscape painfully clear.

But two landscapes in particular involve what the heroine perceives as a direct threat to herself. The first scene involves the violent "mock robbery" of the coach containing Mme. Duval and Evelina by Captain Mirvan and Sir Clement. The second landscape is Vauxhall where Evelina seems threatened by a gang rape on the

---

[3] Jane Austen's earliest works have theatrical influences as well. Of course, her family encouraged amateur theatricals, and Jane Austen wrote plays. Her youthful settings sometimes have a proscenium look.

dark and narrow paths of that pleasure garden. Certainly human actors cause problems for Evelina, but the landscape provides neither prospect to foresee danger nor refuge to escape it.

As with the old women's race, the plan for the mock robbery was described by the two men as "rare sport" with the old French woman. The dehumanization of Mme. Duval seems to be their goal. Captain Mirvan calls the plan "to convoy a crazy vessel to the shore of Mortification" (124), as he depersonalizes her entirely. Even though most of the other women at Howard Grove know of the plot, they keep the secret. These women are threatened themselves and "would not hazard the consequence of discovering his [Mirvan's] designs" (127). Evelina and her grandmother (Mme. Duval) do not have any idea where they are in the landscape. Nothing is known except that the male entourage attending their chariot knows of the plot and cooperates with the two gentlemen, who pretend to be robbers. The only thing the women know for certain is that they are being driven around the countryside for three hours and are totally lost.

Sir Clement comes up to the coach to declare his affection for Evelina and reassure her that the robbery is not real, while Captain Mirvan drags her grandmother off to a ditch, shakes her violently and ties her hand and foot. The reader is left with the image of a poor terrified woman "covered with dirt, weeds, and filth, and her face was really horrible; for the pomatum and powder from her head, and the dust from the road, were quite pasted on her skin by her tears, which, with her rouge, made so frightful a mixture, that she hardly looked human" (134). Mme. Duval describes herself as being pulled and hauled as if she had "no more feeling than a horse" (135). The dehumanizing treatment of a woman as an annoying object in the landscape may have moved the eighteenth-century reader, as it did Evelina, from "laughter at first to irritation with the Captain, for carrying his love of tormenting—*sport* he calls it,—to such barbarous and unjustifiable extremes" (136).

We should note that, during this scene, Evelina and her grandmother are totally unable to recognize any place in the landscape either to hide or to seek. No zone of compromise exists—just unbounded male violence. "The Captain's raptures, during supper, at the success of his plan, were boundless" (137), and his success only encourages him to increase his torment of Mme. Duval, while his own wife fears trying to dissuade him.

The second landscape that seems to veer out of control into hostility toward women (in this case, Evelina herself) is Vauxhall, which Evelina terms "very pretty, but too formal; I should have been better pleased, had it consisted less of straight walks" (178). Although even many male authors of the day found formal gardens old-fashioned, this aspect of Vauxhall does not bode well for Evelina—this landscape implying a certain sense of masculine control as she quotes another poet: "Grove nods at grove, each alley has its brother" (178). Or at least in this landscape, the masculine groves and alleys collude with each other.

Vauxhall, a kind of eighteenth-century equivalent of Coney Island, is full of "deceptions." First, Evelina hears a bell ring and is hurried away to view an artificial cascade by her companions, a group of upstart middle-class friends of Mme. Duval who have no real sense of culture at all and acutely embarrass Evelina. She explains the surprise cascade: "But this was not the only surprise which was to divert them at my expense; for they led me about the garden purposely to enjoy my first sight of various other deceptions" (179). As the two young women of the party taunt Evelina, she follows them down a long, dark alley where they find themselves surrounded by "a large party of gentlemen, apparently very riotous, and who were hallooing, leaning on one another, and laughing immoderately" (180). The men come out from behind some trees and form a circle around the young women, and Evelina observes that "for some minutes we were kept prisoners, till at last one of them, rudely seizing hold of me, said I was a pretty little creature" (181). The men (as in the old women's race and the mock robbery) consider Evelina's attempt to escape down one after the other of the dark alleys as a sport. At each avenue she is confronted with a new pursuer who would hold her in the "most familiar manner" and taunt her by asking to "accompany her in a race" (181), as all the others laughed. She is finally rescued by Sir Clement, who is apparently there to join in the fun of abducting some "loose" young girl who might stray down the path. He has trouble convincing the group that Evelina is not really an actress, or possibly a prostitute; however, he spirits her down an even more desolate alley after he rescues her.

Again, there is no place for a woman to hide or seek in this dark, male-controlled landscape. A landscape that begins as a seemingly innocent, orderly, well-manicured garden turns into a scene with gangs of gentlemen hiding behind the trees and waiting to attack (and probably rape) some unsuspecting woman. An ironic aftermath of this terrible ordeal for Evelina is that the brother of Bid and Poll is more concerned about Evelina's absence because of her naiveté than he is about his sisters, who were still gone. He says: "As long as Miss is come back, I don't mind; for as to Bid and Poll, they can take care of themselves" (185).

If, in these two scenes, Evelina does not remain in danger of experiencing death by landscape, her situation contains a threat similar to that of Atwood's wilderness. The artificial "wilderness" of Vauxhall reveals a scene of neither refuge nor prospect and exposes Evelina to rape—a violent denial of her rights as an individual. What is a "safe place" for a woman, and how can it be recognized aesthetically in literature? How are women able to mediate an aesthetic space for themselves, a zone of compromise of their own? These are important questions we can pose for Burney and Radcliffe's novels, giving us a good idea of the prominent novels and novelistic landscapes by women with which Jane Austen was familiar, but these questions cannot be answered well until we come to Austen's novels. A look at the landscape of *Evelina* and *The Mysteries of Udolpho* allows us to contrast other late eighteenth-century landscapes with Austen's use of aesthetic space, which we will see later. Appleton perceives landscape in some ways that help readers to understand the connections between heroines and place. Although he does not treat women's position in the landscape directly, what he does say about human placement can influence our ideas of feminine aesthetic space.

Before we examine gendered perceptions of landscape in Radcliffe's *The Mysteries of Udolpho*, we need to consider the relationship between society and art. Aesthetic geography provides useful tools for understanding the mediation between these two. "What do we like about landscape, and why do we like it?" asks Appleton. He believes geography needs the arts and that symbolism is the bridge between the requirements for biological survival and sensations derived from the contemplation of landscape. In *The Experience of Landscape*, Appleton proposes a landscape theory which attempts to explain how symbolism bridges the gap between survival in and aesthetic appreciation of the landscape. Appleton's theory analyzes landscape on the basis of habitat ("pleasurable sensations in the experience of landscape to environmental conditions favourable to biological survival" [vii]) and prospect/refuge (landscape perceived in terms of strategic appraisal of the landscape as a potential habitat).

In addition, Appleton concludes that "landscape which affords both a good opportunity to see and a good opportunity to hide is aesthetically more satisfying than one which affords neither" (74). However, he emphasizes that experiencing the landscape aesthetically does not depend directly upon environmental conditions favorable to satisfying primitive needs. The important thing is that the person *thinks* the landscape is favorable.

In his framework of symbolism, Appleton names kinds of prospects, refuges, and hazards in the landscape and how they are interrelated. Restrictions on prospect, even mere "peepholes," the framing of the scene for the heroine, become significant. In other words, how limited the heroine's prospect becomes affects her potential range of action, whether the restriction be a framed landscape painting or a path. Hazards in the landscape present equally important experiences, whether they are incidents or impediments, animate or inanimate, natural or artificial. As Appleton comments, "To 'abolish' hazard altogether is to deprive the prospect and the refuge of their meaningful roles" (96).

A particularly interesting and important kind of balance in the landscape Appleton calls the edge-of-the-wood phenomenon, described as:

> [a woodland] usually depicted with an unenclosed, penetrable edge and often a path, or paths, leading invitingly into the trees. The effect is enhanced by accentuating the details of the symbolism in either half; the prospect is distinguished by clarity, distance and sometimes falling ground, the refuge by an impression of the darkness, depth and capaciousness of the woodland in which the observer can at his own choosing, be swallowed up. (135)

Writers, as well as land managers and painters, strive to tone down the stark contrasts between prospect and refuge that exist in edge-of-the-woods images. Appleton describes the basic solution as the creation of a "zone of compromise," where "the prospect dominant 'voids' spill over into the refuge-dominant 'masses'" (215), so that "the participant can achieve the advantages of good visibility and effective concealment at the same time" (216). A good example of this special zone of compromise, edge-of-the-woods image is Gainsborough's "Cottage Door." The young family have their backs to the open door of the cottage, which is guarded by some tall and sturdy ancient oaks. Through the heavy trees beyond, the viewer can see an open prospect, falling away from their location at the edge of the woods, privileging the cottagers with both a home camouflaged by the forest, yet open to a view of what might approach them.

For Appleton, human experience of the landscape is inbred, evolutionary, and yet socially and culturally learned (and therefore affected by gender). We look back to a nostalgic primeval experience and think of landscape as somehow fulfilling our

Figure 2.1 Thomas Gainsborough, "Cottage Door." Courtesy of Huntington Library, Art Collections, and Botanical Gardens.

biological needs. However, our involvement with symbolic landscape helps us "reconcile the symbolism of our emancipation from the tyranny of environment with the symbolism of that same environment" (173). We find ourselves having a vicarious relationship with an artificial landscape, produced by landscape architects or by novelists.

The advantage of the author over the artist and photographer, however, is that ability to manipulate words to reduplicate landscape symbols, "drawing on vaguely defined but nevertheless powerful associations" (Appleton 213), a reduplication, which calls to mind the narratological palimpsest—a layering of past landscapes. Adding to the complicated layering of images that the author describes is the need for the reader to translate the author's word picture of landscape back into the reader's own spatial experience. So as readers, we do not have the direct experience of a painting or a photograph, but our experience is mediated through words. Additional associations involved in translating add to the palimpsest even more gender-based and psychologically-based perceptions because it is not just how we "see" a landscape, but also how we relate to the language of landscape itself. Although it is impossible to demonstrate with any certainty a correspondence between author, character, and reader's perceptions, a correspondence (or lack of it) can be shown between the author's perception of the landscape and that of the heroine, and part of this correspondence relates to the gender of the author.

The terms used in this study to mediate—settle the "differences"—between women and their literary landscapes reflect Appleton's geographic aesthetics. Lois finds a way, albeit a limited one, in which to deal with landscape, by imagining Lucy still alive in the paintings. Lois creates a zone of compromise. And this zone of compromise is just that—a settlement with both sides conceding. Lois has gained more control over landscape, but she has not "saved" Lucy, and, as a result, Lois can never be totally at ease. Evelina finds herself, when she deviates at all from the paths of culturally prescribed patriarchal control, in a place of extreme hazard, with no refuge or prospect. Prospect, refuge, hazard, zone of compromise, and edge-of-the-wood environments remain terms useful in locating heroines, giving them boundaries or making them aware of the lack of boundaries, as they attempt to find their way in a landscape dominated by a masculine culture. As we examine the landscape of France, Spain, and Italy in Radcliffe's novel, Appleton provides helpful ways of seeing Austen's fictive landscapes.

Published sixteen years after *Evelina*, Ann Radcliffe's *The Mysteries of Udolpho* moves from conventional two-dimensional picturesque scenes to something out-of-control and frightening in a landscape that also seems "haunted" with men. Heroes and villains frequently emerge from Radcliffe's landscape, and the heroine, Emily St. Aubert (she, at least, has a last name), acts occasionally as part of the landscape (insider), as well as controlling viewer of a framed landscape (outsider).

La Vallée, Emily's home in sixteenth-century France, resembles more closely an eighteenth-century scene from the English Lake District—with a rather startling view of the Pyrenees. The landscape description is quite conventionally framed as a picturesque and pastoral two-dimensional work of art, reminiscent of Poussin. But even in this idyllic scene which causes Emily to contemplate God, some unsettling events occur. In the little fishing house, the family's pastoral retreat, Emily hears her own lute being played but cannot discover the player. Also Emily finds that her mother's bracelet containing Emily's miniature has been stolen. Finally a mysterious stranger writes a sonnet on the wainscot calling her "the goddess of the fairy scene," "nymph of these shades" (7). Some male presence in the landscape is inviting Emily to enter into it as an insider too. Although the notion of a mysterious suitor romantically stimulates Emily, the violation of her property unnerves her. In some ways, this stranger's actions are like Evelina's suitor's, meant to be a jest but hinting of potential violation of the heroine's person.

Following the death of her mother, Emily and her father begin a journey through the Pyrenees to Toulouse. Although her father dies early on, her journey continues for the entire novel until she finally returns to La Vallée. The Pyrenees, the Bay of Biscay, the Alps, northern Italy, and the Apennines all provide Radcliffe's heroine with numerous opportunities to use her Claude glass-like descriptive powers. With this framing device, except for the foreground, details are largely lost as the landscape becomes controlled. However in several instances, Emily seems to be a woman involved with a masculine presence in landscape rather than a woman as an intrinsic part of the landscape, one with Nature (as was Lucy of Wordsworth's landscape).

One of Emily's typical views from the "lofty cliffs" of the Pyrenees encompasses a view that moves from mountains to plains to sea in an unbelievable panorama.

> Emily could not restrain her transport as she looked over the pine forests of the mountains upon the vast plains that enriched with woods, towns, blushing vines, and plantations of almonds, palms and olives, stretched along, till their various colours melted in distance into one harmonious hue, that seemed to unite earth with heaven. Through the whole of this glorious scene the majestic Garonne wandered; descending from its source among the Pyrenees, and winding its blue waves towards the Bay of Biscay. (28)

This is typical of one of her landscapes that seem to take in most of the geography of an area (and follows Gilpin's requisite Claude glass scene-making). As a view is sublime—awe-inspiring to the point of creating a *frisson* of potential danger, Radcliffe tells the reader that "this was such a scene as Salvator would have chosen, had he then existed, for his canvas" (30).

Early in the eighteenth century, male tourists and writers (such as Addison) became interested in landscape as they made the Grand Tour part of their experience. However, interest in the Alps and other Continental landscape was gradually displaced by a heightened awareness of English landscape with the country estate serving as a miniature version of the English realm itself. The ideology of the English Park as a special landscape representing English patriotism actually started in the seventeenth century, but the combination of aestheticism and utility, promoted by eighteenth-century landscape artists and architects, combined to valorize the English political system, the private property holder, and a strongly patriarchal culture. In general, the prospect poet's view of the landscape was one which women found difficult to share since they rarely owned property themselves. In fact, they were more likely to be part of the graceful nature reflected in the landscape itself, retaining that "insider" view. With the interest in English rural landscape, improvers, travelers, and writers took on the role of aestheticians as well. These aestheticians insisted on viewing landscape as scenes from the favored

Italian landscape painters of the seventeenth century: Claude Lorrain, Gaspard Poussin (Dughet), and Salvator Rosa. Denis Cosgrove describes the typical Claudian landscape as one "framed by coulisses and leading the eye via a series of highlights to a vanishing point at the horizon" (201). Eighteenth-century landscape architects, artists, and writers all tried endlessly to capture the Arcadian effects of Claude and the mythic images of Poussin in landscapes which frequently duplicated their use of views of Tivoli and the temple of the Sibyl. Rosa exemplified the sublime ideal in rugged landscape. When James Thomson wrote in 1748 in his "Castle of Indolence," "Whate'er Lorrain light-touched with softening hue, Or savage Rosa dashed, or learned Poussin drew," he was revealing a quintessential eighteenth-century prescription for seeing the English landscape. Landscapes by Rosa, in particular, seemed to have heavily influenced Ann Radcliffe's portrayal of the landscape in her novels, since she had not visited the actual landscapes themselves.

The three most influential landscape architects of the eighteenth century, William Kent, Lancelot "Capability" Brown, and Humphry Repton, were clearly influenced by Claude and Poussin. Kent designed the famous grounds of Rousham to resemble a Claudian landscape. Cosgrove describes the view there as based upon a series of recurrent landscape images: "Beginning at the house, the primary view is determined by a wide bowling green stretching away and terminating where the land slopes steeply to the river" (201). The temple of the Sibyl at Stowe is also Kent's design. The mock monastic ruin that he installed on the grounds of one estate seems very much like a painting. This intriguing combination of classical and gothic elements Cosgrove attributes to the general English cultural belief at the time that the English had achieved a "union of the antithetical principle of Roman authority and Gothic liberty," (203) a principle we will later see in Walter Scott's novelistic landscape.

However, Radcliffe's views on Italian and Gothic landscape seem to refute the pride and control of landscape exemplified by these male aestheticians. The landscape of Italy described in *The Mysteries of Udolpho* reflects a morally decadent masculine culture with a sense of freedom that is at once capricious and lawless. The sense of a thoughtful, Roman, law-based society fused with a medieval western European Christianity does not exist here. Such a society is replaced by an atmosphere particularly hostile to any weak but ethical person with a sense of aesthetic integrity, for instance, a woman such as Radcliffe's heroine, Emily.

Lancelot "Capability" Brown carried on Kent's work, which, in many ways, was a reaction to what the English saw as the absolutism of the French system as characterized in the landscape architecture of Versailles. Both Kent and Brown began to incorporate more curves in the landscape. They established painterly views where the ha-has separated the vast lawns from the pasture lands yet allowed the proud English property owner to remind himself of his good husbandry of the land with views of the cattle grazing at an appropriate distance.

As Brown continued this process of mixing the classical with a sense of Gothic freedom, it is important to remember that property rights were open to a very small number of men (and certainly not women). Paternalism marks the English taste for landscape during this period. Brown goes to great length to compare his gardening techniques to literary devices, using landscape as narrative.[4] Brown, more so than his predecessor, composed a unified narrative of his landscape; Christopher Thacker calls it "a single, multi-dimensional composition, in which the contours of the land and the lakes, and the relationship of trees and grassy lawn vary continuously as one walks onwards, experiencing not many different and separated pictorial compositions, but innumerable variations on a single theme" (210). And of course, we might note that this description is not unlike some versions of the newly developing novel form.[5]

Brown's successor, Humphry Repton, might be said to have taken Brown's spare prospects and distances and "prettified" them. Toward the end of the century, the theory of the picturesque became more prominent in landscape design, and Repton interpreted this theory as one generally favoring asymmetrical landscapes with less order and congruity than those of Brown. (As did Brown, Repton wrote a great deal about his theory of art and its application to the landscape.) Most interesting (and satirized by Jane Austen in *Mansfield Park*) were his large books of "before" and "after" landscapes. His "improved" views remove any unsightly huts, beggars in the flower garden, or vulgar butcher shops. Repton writes that a painter "sees things as they are; the landscape gardener as they will be" (Hipple 233). Later, we will examine Repton and Austen's similarities in treatment of landscape. Austen could both poke fun at Repton yet admire some of his landscapes as well.

Repton admired Edmund Burke's *Philosophical Enquiry into the Origin of our Ideas of the Sublime and Beautiful* (1757), and Burke's perceptions of the sublime and beautiful greatly influenced improvers (as well as aestheticians), many of whom used his theories as a basis for a landscape which provided a compromise between the sublime and beautiful.[6] Edmund Burke, in many ways, acts as a bridge between earlier eighteenth-century aesthetic views and those of the later half of the century and beyond. His philosophy of politics (as well as morality and economy) might be described as "organic." If change is to occur in any area, it is only fitting that this change be slow and evolving as a "natural" outgrowth of what he saw as God's law. And, of course, this was best exemplified in "natural" English liberty. The aristocracy, the gentry, and the lower classes all should know their duties and responsibilities, and any changes therein must necessarily be very gradual. Women and peasants needed to be valued and taken care of, as did the landscape.

When Burke began to explore aesthetic taste, he saw the Sublime as directly related to the human urge for self-preservation. Experienced at a safe distance, the Sublime, according to Burke, can be quite exhilarating—giving the spectator a "*frisson* of terror," as in a Rosa landscape. Burke shows how a primary fear for one's physical safety can be transposed to the vicarious excitement of a narrow escape from danger—that edge-of-the-wood feeling Appleton discusses. As long as pain

---

[4] See *English Landscaping and Literature, 1660-1840* (NY: Oxford UP, 1966) by Edward Malins for more on landscape as narrative.

[5] In fact, Appleton comments on the process of the writer and reader dealing with landscape in this way: "The great advantage of the writer is that, since his landscape pictures have to be coded into words and then decoded by the reader into pictures, there are two opportunities for the enrichment of the landscape by the imagination" (214).

[6] See Walter J. Hipple, Jr. *The Beautiful, the Sublime and the Picturesque in Eighteenth-century British Aesthetic Theory*. Carbondale, Ill: Southern Ill UP, 1957.

and danger do not press too closely, we feel curiosity and sympathy. Radcliffe's heroine, Emily, experiences the equivalent of Burke's sublime in the rugged mountain prospect views that she describes in the Pyrennes and the mountains of Italy. These views are sublime as long as she feels a God-inspired fear and awe in the vastness of the scene without immediate danger.

On the opposite end of the aesthetic spectrum, Burke deals with what he perceives as the Beautiful.[7] As the Sublime is related to self-preservation, the Beautiful is related to society. Beauty is a social quality related to physical passion, tender sentiments, sympathy, and "a growing reliance of feeling as a means of insight." Burke's idea of the beautiful is exemplified in *The Mysteries of Udolpho* by the little fishing house and its diminutive serene surrounding at La Vallée or the small *hortus conclusus*—secret garden—where Emily meets her lover. Although Burke's theory was not intended solely as a means of describing landscape, it remained heavily influential in that area throughout the rest of the century.

Burke's Sublime and Beautiful, while compelling for artists and improvers, left a large space between the two qualities of landscape, which the Reverend William Gilpin strove to fill. The Picturesque—"that beauty which is agreeable in a picture" (Watkins 75)—filled the space. During what has been called the picturesque decade of the 1790s, the highest praise for a landscape was to say it resembled a painting. During his travels through England, Gilpin developed a theory for seeing nature as art. If the property owners seemed to control landscape economically and aesthetically earlier in the century, the advent of tourism and the "search for the picturesque" made commodification of the landscape even more apparent.[8] "Scene-hopping" became very popular with tourists, who took Gilpin's books along for their illustrative landscape pictures to make sure they viewed the scene from the correct angle and mentally edited out of the picture any feature they were not "supposed" to see.

A real concern for framing and perspective becomes noticeable when one realizes the number of traveling "knick-knacks" required of the fashionable late eighteenth-century landscape viewer. Besides the sketchbooks and journals, the up-to-date tourist on tour would probably carry a Claude glass. However, Gilpin and the picturesque tourists were, by means of the Claude glass, able to "appropriate natural scenery and process it into a commodity ... convert[ing] nature's unmanageable bounty into a frameable possession," according to Andrews (81). Anything outside the frame had a questionable existence. The predominantly masculine, patriarchal, controlling position of the landscape basically excluded women as spectators (unless of course they wished to take up their Claude glasses, as many women did, and tour the landscape using the proper masculine perspective). Even when, as some proto-romantics did toward the end of the century, these male prospect-viewers got down into the landscape, they were not *of* it; they simply went from reasoning control of it to an imaginative control of the landscape.

However, some critics have concluded that the picturesque became a liberating landscape for women in that it is detached from the patriarchal historical scenes of

---

[7] Later critics have occasionally commented that Burke's list of adjectives describing what is beautiful seem to indicate that he is thinking of his wife, i.e. small, smooth, delicate.

[8] See Malcolm Andrews' *The Search for the Picturesque: Landscape, Aesthetics, and Tourism in Britain, 1760-1800* (Stanford: Stanford UP, 1989) for a more complete study of picturesque scenery as commodity.

previous landscapes. W. C. Snyder believes that "critically and historically, then, the picturesque opens women artists to participation in a specific artistic program embracing values with which they could identify and feel free to express" (160). He adds that the picturesque contains "a strain in the movement which leans toward care and preservation (the feministic), without an imagery of procreation and fertility (the materialistic)" (161). Jill Heydt-Stevenson, who has studied extensively the connections between Austen and the picturesque, writes:

> In Austen's novels, arguments about the construction of a national identity converge with arguments about the construction of womanhood and the construction of landscape. When we examine this convergence, we find that Austen explores the junction between the boundaries of personal liberty allowed to women and those allowed to the landscape itself, privileging for her own heroines bonds with the wilder, unornamented, picturesque landscape. (261)

So, even though women writers were aware of the proprietor gaze on the landscape, Radcliffe, and later Austen, found ways of using the picturesque views of the landscape to their advantage. Radcliffe paints landscapes, which contain both masculine and feminine images.

It certainly will not surprise the reader who realizes the strong presence of the male spectator that, after Emily is separated from her true love, Valancourt, she associates most of the landscape she sees on her journey with him, and a mysterious male presence (as at the fish house at La Vallée) again suffuses the landscape. In Toulouse, where she is forbidden to see him by her aunt, he says, "I have haunted this place—these gardens, for many—many nights, with a faint, very faint hope of seeing you" (152). Later, the sublimity of the Alps "sometimes banished the idea of Valancourt, though they more frequently revived it" (163). The landscape seems to affect her psychically. As she is confined in Udolpho, or some other castle prison, she frequently hears music off in the distance at night and associates it with Valancourt. In any case, she seems to attach this male presence to her own in order to retain the eighteenth-century male spectator view.

However, Emily's views cease to be either sublime or picturesque under two different circumstances. One involves a recurrent reverie she has during which she imagines herself as a sea-nymph. The other occurs when Emily is forced to go with henchmen from Udolpho into an unframed, terrifying situation that is all hazard and no refuge. As a result of her dream of a seascape, Emily composes a poem called "The Sea-Nymph" where the ultimate refuge for a maid like her is under the sea.

> In coral bow'rs I love to lie,
> And hear the surges roll above,
> And through the waters view on high
> The proud ships sail, and gay clouds move. (179)

As a sea-nymph, woman has the ultimate place to hide and place to seek.[9] She can "dance upon the lapsing tides" or "seek [her] crystalcourt,/ deep in the wave, 'mid

---

[9] In Charlotte Brontë's *Villette*, Lucy has similar dreams of safety under the sea. But Charlotte Brontë also brings a terrible woman out of the sea to revenge herself on the lover who spurned her in Brontë's poem "Gilbert."

Neptune's woods" (180). Her only encounter with hazard involves saving drowning seamen (when Neptune permits).

If we consider eighteenth-century landscape as representing Gothic liberty and Roman authority, both of these aspects are certainly absent from the unframed terrifying landscape that confronts Emily outside of the castle at Udolpho. Emily is in no sense free (except in her aesthetic ability to frame the landscape), and authority in Italy at this time appears to be entirely in the hands of the local ruffians. This landscape seems to Emily as full of banditti as Vauxhall was swarming with lechers for Evelina. As in the scenes from Burney's novel, this scene is obscure, with no place to hide or seek and every reason for the heroine to believe she will be raped or murdered. "Toward evening, they wound down precipices, black with forests of cypress, pine and cedar, into a glen so savage and secluded, that if Solitude ever had local habitation, this might have been 'her place of dearest residence.' To Emily it appeared a spot exactly suited to the retreat of banditti" (402). The men do not murder her only because the evil owner of Udolpho does not give this command, but we know they are certainly capable of doing so, and the landscape feels full of a dangerous male presence which might easily violate any woman, just as Burney's more satiric landscapes might. As with Evelina, no zone of compromise exists for the heroine. Even when the cutthroats arrive at an idyllic cottage on the edge of the wood—one that would ordinarily fit all of Appleton's requirements for a perfect zone of compromise—Emily finds out it is just another temporary prison for her until they can take her back to Udolpho.

Neither Evelina nor Emily exists in the landscape with true safety. The women writers of these two novels, *Evelina* and *The Mysteries of Udolpho*, vacillate between trying the old male spectator approach and having their heroines lose control in a landscape full of potentially violent men. Not only do these women have little control of their landscape, they are also exploited, in Evelina's case, for her vulnerability in having no fixed name or property, and in Emily's case, for her property. In both cases the heroines *are* the property, the commodities, and yet the authors (even though they are women) feel forced to follow the controlling eighteenth-century male property owners' traditional view of the landscape. No wonder women sometimes become confused and lose their control of the landscape.

Of course, the changes occurring in the landscapes of these novels reflect some of the incipient Romantic attitudes which also influenced Wordsworth and Coleridge, and the interest in what these authors see as nature, untouched by artifice, is not unique to their gender. However, the ambivalence over who controls the landscape and the potential danger of a male presence there trying to objectify women and convert them into property appear as themes in both these novels by women, the reverberations of which are felt by women fiction writers up to the present. As girls at a camp in southern Canada, Atwood's female characters are well aware that when they pretended to be Indian braves exploring the Canadian wilderness, eventually their femininity would be exposed to the dangers of being consumed by the landscape. Searching for prospects and refuges in the landscape of Jane Austen involves an increasing awareness of women negotiating the pitfalls and hazards in their landscape. The young women in Austen's youthful pieces faint and then die "of landscape," so to speak, but also build a natural sanctuary—a place to hide and a place from which to seek. As Radcliffe, then Austen, and, much later,

Atwood, struggle to frame the landscape in stories, they give their female protagonists a chance to avoid the possibility of "stepping aside" and becoming lost forever.

In the next chapter, we will look at Jane Austen's earliest attempts at using landscape. In these youthful fictional pieces, Austen's awareness of how landscape affects heroines may the surprise the reader. Her satire on landscape and how men and women respond to it ranges from the four equally spaced cows that Mr. Gower in "Evelyn" admired to the bower that provides a place of solace for Kitty in "Catharine,—Or The Bower." The advice we come away with from one of her most extended pieces, "Love and Freindship," on how to behave in the landscape is fairly simple: "Run mad as often as you choose; but do not faint" (122). Thus may a heroine avoid "death by landscape."

Chapter 3

"Four White Cows Disposed at Equal Distances"—or—Steel Traps to Bowers in Austen's Short Fiction

> At the start of the nineteenth century ... it became possible for a clergyman's daughter who spent her life in a few confined spaces to realize her immense talents by seeing that she had, within those spaces, materials rich enough to challenge her. Particular place was all, and Austen herself knew this, if only instinctively.
>
> (Sales, *Closer to Home* 63)

Jane Austen's short fiction surprises most readers, who usually discover her youthful pieces when they continue their search for more Austen to read after the six novels. Instead of finding the subtlety, restraint, and understatement of her mature works, they are startled to find, as Juliet McMaster puts it in "The Short Fiction: Energy Versus Sympathy," "boisterous overstatement [which] is not just over the top, but down the other side too" (175). McMaster also notices that "the young Jane Austen was still relatively free of gendered identity, and she presents characters who are similarly unsocialized" (176). Victorian relatives of Jane Austen hesitated at publishing these, for them, faintly embarrassing, albeit exuberant, youthful pieces.[1] Other readers, such as novelist Reginald Hill, believe that the short fiction *is* the lens through which to read all of Jane Austen's later work properly.[2]

Margaret Anne Doody claims, in *The Cambridge Companion to Jane Austen*, that Austen's youthful efforts were the kind of writing she really wanted to do—short, fantastic, eighteenth-century tales, "light and bright and sparkling." Doody also contends that what Austen wanted to write didn't fit with Regency publishers' notions of what a Regency audience wanted in a novel. "The obstreperous qualities that work well in short fiction were not highly valued in the novel" (92), and short fiction was not as popular in the early nineteenth century as it had been fifty years earlier. So as Austen became more aware of a reading audience beyond her familiar circle of family and friends, she eventually adapted her material so that it would suit publishers' demands.

What does Jane Austen's adolescent lack of publishing savvy have to do with her use of landscape? In fact, a reader, upon first encountering Jane Austen's short fiction, might be surprised that these short pieces, with their exaggerated

---

[1] In fact, they all were not published until R.W. Chapman gradually made them public between 1923 and 1954.

[2] See "Jane Austen: A Voyage of Discovery" in *Persuasions* (19), 77-92.

characterization and abrupt endings, would pay attention to landscape at all. However, any examination of her early writing reveals a surprising variety of socially constructed landscapes that are even clearer in their unvarnished juvenile prose than they are in her mature work. Just as her characters and plots are exaggerated versions of what she later refined and toned down for the novel-reading expectations of the time, so her early landscape sketches are exaggerated and reveal the raw intensity which exhibited itself more subtly in her later works. Doody comments insightfully on the young Jane Austen's treatment of landscape, society, and gender:

> Austen's early fiction is a mock-pastoral world in which eviscerated institutions, or institutionalized ideas, though sometimes honoured in gesture, are unable to contain the characters' curiosity, animation, or general desire for self-gratification ... The law of the Father is a kind of gesture in the air. (92)

The notion of a palimpsest shows here—the pastoral scene visible beneath the more realistic eighteenth-century drawing room image, the expected conventionally masculine landscape occasionally usurped by a girl.

The idea of a landscape telling a story, represented in the landscapes of Brown and Kent, are reflected in young Austen's scenes. Christopher Thacker in his *History of Gardens* describes an estate, designed by a landscape architect, aiming to project a narrative onto the landscape:

> At Stourhead, when the form of the gardens was established, the instructed visitor was meant to perambulate in a certain direction, following and receiving a succession of hints and statements provided by grotto, inscription, urn and temple which alluded to episodes in Virgil's *Aeneid*. (194)

As we examine some of Austen's earliest scenes, we can imagine the characters walking the paths, following a typical circuit around a landscaped estate of Brown or Kent.

Landscape figures prominently in "Frederic and Elfrida," written by Jane Austen when she was about twelve. Here the landscape echoes the kind of eighteenth-century fantastical tales Austen had no doubt read in her father's library. Frederic and Elfrida find themselves in Crankhumdunberry "of which sweet village [Charlotte's] father was rector" (*MW* 5). Frederic and Elfrida "proposed to her to take a walk in a grove of poplars, which led from the parsonage to a verdant lawn, enamelled with a variety of variegated flowers, and watered by a purling stream, brought from the Valley of Tempé by a passage under ground" (5). Suddenly two young women appear, singing a song about a "Damon," who is in love with them, and then the singers disappear—figures receding into the landscape. Definitely this notion of mock pastoral operates in combination with Austen's idea of a landscape where women have the power to appear and disappear at will.

In this pastoral scene, the young women are described as "elegant," yet as they immediately go to visit these "amiable and worthy Girls" (6), Frederic and Elfrida exclaim to one of them (incongruously):

> Lovely and too charming fair one, notwithstanding your forbidding squint, your greasy tresses, and your swelling back which are more frightful than imagination can paint or pen

describe, I cannot refrain from expressing my raptures at the engaging qualities of your mind, which so amply atone for the horror with which your first appearance must ever inspire the unwary visitor. (6)

So the twelve-year-old Jane Austen shows the contrast between the ideal (patriarchal) pastoral landscape where the girls are supposed to resemble beautiful nymphs and the reality of the parlor scene where only the girl's mind may be admired, in sharp contrast with her unattractive exterior—ironic, probably because even the young Jane Austen recognizes that most people cannot admire the clever mind housed in an unattractive body. Even in this early piece, Austen seems to recognize all the difference the setting can make in seeing the figure.

Later, Charlotte, who introduces Frederic and Elfrida to this landscape, decides herself to "become one with it." After spurning convention in accepting the proposals of two men at once, she shows her remorse by throwing herself into a deep stream and floating down to Crankhumdunberry, "where she was picked up and buried" (9). The narrator then proceeds to instruct the reader concerning the appropriate emotions to feel when reading Charlotte's tombstone, concerning her throwing "her sweet body and her lovely face/ Into the stream that runs through Portland Place." The narrator asserts that if the reader does not cry at these words, "Your mind must be unworthy to peruse them" (9).

Even in this early piece, Austen is pointing to the cultural construction of women as part of the landscape. In the closed society of their houses, the women are presented realistically (if unpleasantly), with greasy hair or with the dilemma of a double engagement. But as they enter the idealistic landscape of Sensibility, they become nymphs, singing magically or performing the quintessential act of becoming one with the landscape in death. At twelve, Jane knows exactly what landscape means in art and how women are meant to behave in the landscape. And she also knows how to poke fun at that tradition.

In her short fiction, Austen also shows women trapped by their landscape. The hapless Lucy of "Jack and Alice" finds herself "caught in one of the steel traps so common in gentlemen's grounds" (22). (Again, the reader might remember Wordsworth's Lucy, who dies, becoming one with the landscape, as well as Atwood's Lucy, trapped in Lois's landscape paintings.) Austen's Lucy has arrived on the scene while pursuing the cruel and totally indifferent Charles and trespassing on his estate. Austen describes a male-dominated estate, one which is not a landscape upon which a young woman might move with impunity, but here heroines generally asserted themselves in surprisingly uncharacteristic ways for that time. It appears that Charles Adams has had his property deliberately sown with steel traps to keep out unwanted female admirers (just as bad as poachers, in his eyes). After all, we find out early on that Charles Adams is quite desirable, "of so dazzling a beauty that none but eagles could look him in the face" (13). However, though Lucy is punished for trespassing, a feminine transformative experience does take place in this seemingly hostile environment. After Lucy (still caught in the trap) tells her story, Lady Williams easily sets Lucy's leg, and they all walk back to Lady Williams's house, none the worse for the experience.

As a precocious adolescent, Jane Austen recognized, from her considerable experience in reading, and somewhat less in socializing, that men controlled the landscape. Male "improvers" seeded the grounds with steel traps and erected the park palings. Either they controlled it artistically, with women becoming idealized nymphs and sad suicidals, or they controlled it more overtly as in "Amelia Webster," a very short series of letters, where Benjamin Bar suggests that he and Sally correspond by placing their letters in "a very convenient old hollow oak" (48). He explains to her that, even though the tree is very far from her and much closer to him, he "considered that the walk would be of benefit to [her] in [her] weak and uncertain state of health" and he "preferred it to one nearer [her] home" (48). Sally, it appears, has very little to say about the location of the tree. Place is everything here, and the "joke" involves the complete powerlessness of the girl in its selection. This little piece says a great deal about the assumptions of the gentleman landscape owner and proprietor about his position and the position of any woman (or girl).

The pieces to which I have previously referred are part of Volume I of Austen's "Juvenilia." "Love and Freindship" (Volume II) and "Evelyn" (Volume III), two later pieces, contrast women and men and their relationship to the landscape in even greater detail. In "Love and Freindship," another "death by landscape" takes place. Here, Austen takes a stereotypical landscape of sensibility and exposes it, giving it a humorous twist and allowing the heroine to recognize her ability to control what happens within the landscape. At one point in this story, Sophia and Laura are welcomed into the home of a friend, where they are not exactly the most exemplary of guests. After meddling egregiously in the affairs of their host and even stealing money from him, Laura and Sophia are finally evicted from the estate. They then wander down the road for a mile and a half and "sat down by the side of a clear, limpid stream ... [a] place ... suited for meditation." Austen's description of "a grove of full-grown elms" juxtaposed with "a bed of full-grown nettles" (97) immediately causes us to smile at the idea of its being a "place of meditation." She continues her satire on sensibility as she tells the story of Sophia, continually upset with the aspects of the scene that remind her of her lost husband: "What a beautiful sky! Do not thus distress me by calling my attention to an object which so cruelly reminds me of my Augustus's blue satin Waistcoat" (98). After finding their husbands (about whom, previously, they had almost forgotten) fatally injured in a wrecked phaeton, Sophia faints and Laura runs mad, shouting gibberish in the manner of King Lear: "'They told me my Edward was not Dead; but they deceived me—they took him for a Cucumber" (100). Finally both young women reach a white cottage "amidst the Grove of Elms" (100), very similar to the little cottage in the woods image mentioned by Appleton, one which is a place of refuge—a place to hide and a place from which to seek.[3] Here, taking refuge, the heroine, Laura, learns that she has actually handled herself in her landscape in a way that saves her, unlike the

---

[3] In *Living Space in Fact and Fiction* (Routledge, 1989), Phillipa Tristram discusses cottages and their place in fiction. She writes that their purpose reassures "even the most genteel with a sense of arrival, so that the wanderer feels instantly 'at home'" (1). Tristram comments on Austen's satirization of "cottage taste" in much of her writing from her *Juvenilia,* but mainly Austen objects to pretension and dishonesty in connection with the middle class and the cottage ornée. Austen satirizes cottages in her very early work, "A Tale," in her honeysuckle-covered cottage in *Sense and Sensibility* on through her last work, *Sanditon.*

unfortunate Sophia. On her deathbed, Sophia makes Laura aware of how well she has actually survived the landscape, explaining:

> One fatal swoon has cost me my life. ... Beware of swoons, dear Laura ... A frenzy fit is not one quarter so pernicious; it is an exercise to the body and if not too violent, is I dare say, conducive to health in its consequences. Run mad as often as you choose; but do not faint. (102)

And thus Jane Austen indirectly counsels her female readers how to avoid death by landscape.

Wordsworth moves in another direction. Marlon Ross makes an astute observation about Wordsworth's male and female characters and their relation to nature. He asserts: "Wordsworth's Nature-identified men are not figures absorbed by natural force, limited to the present, arrested by unself-consciousness the way his women are" (407). Ross then asks "And where does this leave the female in Wordsworth's landscape? Where she already has been before Wordsworth began to write: delimited not only by assumed natural boundaries, but also by overriding male desire, whose prerogatives claim all territory as its own" (408). At least Laura escapes being absorbed by nature and losing her life to the landscape in the way Sophia and Wordsworth's Lucy do. Austen recognizes another path for female characters.

No running mad about the landscape for the hero of her later juvenile piece, "Evelyn," written when Jane Austen was fifteen. In fact, in "Evelyn," the main character, Mr. Gower, readily appropriates the landscape around him, and, if he finds it problematic, he simply closes his eyes as he rides through the darkness. Evelyn is a village described by Austen as "perhaps one of the most beautiful Spots in the south of England" (180). Mr. Gower immediately comes upon a small estate directly out of a picturesque landscape painting, with everything neatly and symmetrically arranged down to the last cow:

> As he approached the House, he was delighted with its situation. It was in the exact centre of a small circular paddock, which was enclosed by a regular paling, and bordered with a plantation of Lombardy poplars, and Spruce firs alternatively placed in three rows. A gravel walk ran through this beautiful Shrubbery, and as the remainder of the paddock was unencumbered with any other Timber, the surface of it perfectly even & smooth, and grazed by four white Cows which were disposed at equal distances from each other. (181)

Charlotte Bronte, in an oft-quoted letter to George Lewes, criticizes Austen for her decidedly manicured, formulaic settings: "A carefully fenced, highly cultivated garden, with neat borders and delicate flowers; but no glance of bright vivid physiognomy, no open country, no fresh air, no blue hill, no bonny beck" (1179-80). However, Brian Southam finds the description of the Webb family home as "regular and meticulous enumeration, a satire upon the layout of the formal garden, by then outmoded, and also upon the elaboration of inconsequential detail" (*Literary Manuscripts* 37). Here a fifteen-year-old girl illustrates what landscape the typical Englishman saw as a "picture of perfection" (and probably one that made Jane feel "sick and wicked"). Even as a very young writer, Jane Austen was capable of recognizing and satirizing the stereotypical set piece of the typical landscape artists of the time. On some level, the young Austen recognized what Ross has noted about the male writer, such as Wordsworth: the male spectator gets to claim the territory he desires as his own.

Mr. Gower basically need do nothing more than ask for the property, and the owners happily hand it over to him, including their lovely daughter (also considered "property"). Mr. Gower later "recollects" that when he arrived in Evelyn, he was on a mission to get a portrait of his sister's deceased fiancé for her. As Mr. Gower approaches the castle of the dead man's parents, he is faced with a sublime scene, contrasting sharply with his new picturesque home, and it frightens him. "The gloomy appearance of the old Castle frowning on him as he followed its' winding approach, struck him with terror" (187). However, he prefers his landscapes less awesome. Unlike Laura and Sophia, who run mad or faint, as Mr. Gower rode away on horseback, "he felt indeed almost distracted with his fears, and shutting his Eyes till he arrived at the Village to prevent his seeing either Gipsies or Ghosts, he rode on a full gallop all the way" (189).

So far, in Austen's youthful landscape descriptions, we see an authorial consciousness of the conventional artistic landscapes of the day and the conventional attitude men and women had toward the landscapes. In *Closer to Home: Writers and Place in England*, Roger Sales discusses how Austen's use of place changes from her early novels, where "place is an idea, stated but unembodied" (39) to her later works which "saturate us in a place to such an extent that it can feel like the whole world" (53). This argument is even more clearly illustrated in Austen's short fiction where her landscape is heavily influenced by her reading of the novels of Charlotte Smith, as well as by reading Gilpin's books on travel.[4] Women die and become one with the landscape; men can appropriate landscape fairly easily, seeding it with traps, choosing the most convenient hollow oak, or simply asking for the most unimaginatively bland and pretty estate they stumble upon. If a man finds himself threatened by a frightening scene, he just closes his eyes until any unpleasantness passes. The woman successfully surviving the landscape must at least work herself into a fine kind of madness.

The excess and overstatement of much of Austen's youthful fiction and subversion of conventional gender attitudes, suggested by Juliet McMaster in "The Short Fiction: Energy versus Sympathy," actually accentuates the consequences for unself-consciously bold female characters as they interact with landscape. However, we have yet to come upon those "betwixt and between" moments, where landscape helps liberate a character from societal restraints—even transgress or transform space—beyond Lucy's fortunate escape from the mantrap. Men already own the landscape. If we need more evidence of this social construct, we need only examine Mr. Andrews in the Gainsborough portrait, "Mr. And Mrs. Robert Andrews" (1748-50), cockily leaning against the tree holding his gun and surveying his estate, or Charles Adams and his traps; it is women who must find a way to use landscape to their advantage—to hide and seek—and—with any luck, prevail.[5]

---

[4] See Brian Southam's "A Critical Study of the Short Fiction" in *Jane Austen's Literary Manuscripts* (Oxford: Oxford U P, 1964).

[5] Gillian Rose's *Feminism and Geography: The Limits of Geographical Knowledge* (U of Minnesota P, 1993) contains one of the best critiques of the Gainsborough painting, "Mr. and Mrs. Andrews." Rose describes the celebration of ownership portrayed here and the role of Mr. Andrews and

Figure 3.1 Thomas Gainsborough, "Mr. and Mrs. Andrews," (1748-50). Courtesy National Gallery. Bought with contributions from the Pilgrim Trust, the National Art Collections Fund, Associated Television Ltd, and Mr. and Mrs. W. W. Spooner, 1960.

Jane Austen's dedication of "Evelyn" is dated May 1792; her dedication of "Catharine,—Or The Bower" is dated the following August. However, landscape is dealt with rather differently in the later piece than it is in the earlier one. Evelyn is a stereotypically pretty village that basically acts as a nice repository for the passive Mr. Gower. In "Catharine,—Or The Bower," Kitty, along with the help of her girl friends, builds her own bower and uses it in a variety of ways, some of which act to educate her and others to liberate her. Kitty's bower provides her with the means to transform and transgress space in ways that Austen's later heroines, such as Emma Woodhouse and Anne Elliot, bring into fuller use.

Just as Elizabeth, Fanny, Emma, and Anne later found "consolation" in the landscape, so fifteen-year-old Kitty finds her bower, "work of her own infantine labours" (137), to

> possess such a charm over her senses as constantly to tranquillize her mind and quiet her spirits. Solitude and reflection might perhaps have the same effect in her bed chamber, yet habit had so strengthened the idea which fancy had first suggested, that such a thought never occurred to Kitty, who was firmly persuaded that her bower alone could restore her to herself. (137)

So the bower became a repository of her past for Kitty, a layering of fond memories for her to review.

Kitty's bower was the place where she spent much time in recalling happier childhood days with her two friends. She was close to home there, yet the bower was a place she could go to get away from her overly protective aunt, who thought that the dampness of the bower was conducive to illness. Generally, when the close, confining society of the parlor became too much for her, she had her escape, ruminating on how the Wynnes had mistreated the friends who had helped her build the bower:

> She then left the room; and running out of the house, was soon in her dear bower, where she could indulge in peace all her affectionate anger against the relations of the Wynnes, which was greatly heightened by finding from Camilla that they were in general considered as having acted particularly well by them-, She amused herself for some time in abusing and hating them all with great spirit; and when this tribute to her regard for the Wynnes was paid, and the bower began to have its usual influence over her spirits, she contributed towards settling them by taking out a book, for she had always one about her, and reading. (149)

In a similar way, Anne Elliot, in *Persuasion*, coped with the irritations of her family in the confines of her home. Anne also had a garden to go to and a hedgerow to hide in and reflect on the unfairness of life. As Anne grew older that retreat became a place of stagnation—a trap—but for a teenaged girl like Kitty, her retreat was ideal. The bower was neither in the confining space of the house nor was it part

---

his freedom of movement on his estate. Rose writes, "Mr. Andrews is represented as the owner of the land, while Mrs. Andrews is painted almost as a part of that still and exquisite landscape" (93). Also one may note that Gainsborough left a blank spot on the newly-wed Mrs. Andrews' lap for the expected future son.

of the wild unknown. It was, in fact, that perfect aesthetic landscape, providing a place to hide and yet a place to seek, a space where a girl—or woman—might have the chance to stand at the threshold of freedom from societal restraints.

Such a landscape seems "only natural," yet it actually is not. The bower was carefully and lovingly constructed by three girls working together. Now its construction stands as a monument to the two girls who are caught up in what Jane Austen might consider a kind of gender servitude, one forced to go to India and marry a rich, much older man she didn't love (as Jane Austen's Aunt Philadelphia had actually done) and the other forced to act as a companion and treated as a poor relation. Although her aunt constantly threatens to tear the bower down, Kitty knows she will not because her aunt recognizes its importance to Kitty's well-being. In many ways, this landscape is a way of imposing control on the environment by turning it into an aesthetic structure—one where the female has some power. Instead of being an obvious set piece, constructed strictly to satirize attitudes to landscape, the bower begins to move toward the status Sales claims for Austen's later landscape, such as Mansfield Park which, he suggests, "can teach better than its inhabitants" (46). As Cresswell notes, space/place is used to question the normative world, and what Kitty and her friends have done is really an act of transgression. Kitty's aunt realizes the transgressive nature of the bower but is too kind (and ineffectual) to do anything about it.

The bower really does put Kitty in an interesting "betwixt and between" landscape "when people are disposed to feel liberated from the norms of their society" (Ringer 22). The bower is one of the first of many outdoor settings Jane Austen uses to allow her heroines free conversation with their suitors, away from any prying parental ears. In fact, Jeffrey Herrle in his "Introduction" to "Catharine,—Or The Bower" comments that the bower "becomes a sexualized place, where girlhood and womanhood converge" (ix), and so it seems to fit in that "betwixt and between" landscape. As Herrle aptly puts it: The bower can be monitored by Mrs. Percival, yet outsiders are free to visit it. It is "the creative product of social effort and a social threshold" (x).

Austen tells us that Kitty and Edward Stanley are left "together in the arbour to wander alone to some other part of the garden, to eat the fruit, and examine Mrs. Percival's greenhouse" (169). In this scene, the bower acts as a space where Kitty can transgress boundaries of propriety without really hurting anyone or getting hurt herself, as she practices being an adult. Because Kitty is accustomed to thoughtful pursuits in her bower, she engages Edward in an historical discussion. Having no firm opinions of his own, he is, of course, very entertaining as he can take either side of the issue and argue it.

He stages a mock fit of passion, grasping Kitty's hand and then suddenly dashing off as he sees Mrs. Percival approach, just to provoke the older woman. Overly protective of Kitty and worried about her own health, Mrs. Percival acts as a precursor to Mr. Woodhouse and his hypochondria. She accuses Kitty of being "*profligate* as I *knew* you to be" (170) and reiterates her threat to have the bower "pulled down." Kitty defends herself, and her aunt then seems to forget about Kitty's honor as Mrs. Percival becomes much more concerned over getting a cold in the damp air.

The bower is the focal point of this short work by Austen. Kitty uses it as a place to hide and reflect on her friends' misfortunes. She uses it as a place to read and seek knowledge of the world. She goes to her bower to retreat from the suffocating overprotection of her aunt and the irritating remarks of Camilla and Mrs. Stanley. And finally she uses the bower to transgress social boundaries (after all, a bower is sometimes defined as a boudoir) just a little as she enters the adult world of male/female relationships. However, in some ways the bower has transformative power as well. It is in the bower that she recognizes that, just because Edward has the outward trappings of a potential suitor, it is unreasonable "to suppose that a young man would be seriously attached in the course of four and twenty hours to a girl who has nothing to recommend her but a good pair of eyes" (174). Like Elizabeth Bennet, Kitty also has the "good pair of eyes," but Kitty does a quicker realistic appraisal of Edward's sincerity and potential commitment than some of Austen's later heroines are able to do (Elizabeth and Wickham, Emma and Frank Churchill). In the end, "the bower alone retained its interest in her feelings, and perhaps that was owing to the particular remembrance it brought to her mind of Edward Stanley" (177). The bower has been transformed from a place of childhood memories to a prospect on incipient male/female relationships for Kitty. A new layer has been added to the palimpsest of this landscape—one of awakening sexuality and womanhood, and the bower has proved to be a zone of safety in which Kitty can experience this new awareness.

Brian Southam in "A Critical Study of the Short Fiction," claims that Jane Austen's earliest work significantly influenced her novels. He writes that "'Evelyn' may have been a trifle thrown off to amuse the family but, no less than the obvious and ambitious experiments, it is a working out of certain ideas and methods which were to contribute to her design in the mature works" (38). Prominent among these ideas and methods were her early notions of what landscapes meant to her heroines and how they could use them to their advantage. Kitty is a kind of "heroine-in-training." She does not end up with a husband, but she learns, not from a mother figure, but from her surroundings, how to handle herself in social situations. As we examine her earliest novels, *Susan*, published posthumously as *Northanger Abbey*, *Elinor and Marianne*, later called *Sense and Sensibility*, and *First Impressions*, later *Pride and Prejudice*, we will see how Jane Austen creates a transformative feminine way of looking at the landscape. The heroines of these full-fledged novels move beyond the light flirtation of Kitty's bower to the eventual conclusion of all comic novels—a happy marriage. Austen's landscape also moves from the satiric scenes of her adolescent work to the fiction of the last few months of her life, leading Southam to comment, "Ultimately, in *Sanditon*, the setting becomes an agent in the story, a considerable element in the meaning of the work" (*Literary Manuscripts* 38).

Chapter 4

Heroines-in-Training: The First Three

> If, as Hegel suggests, the act of experiencing is a double act in which we constitute both self and object, then how we see ourselves will be inextricably linked with how we see the world. Our views both of ourselves and of the world will be interpretations rather than essential truths, and these interpretations will be the creations of an activity that constitutes self and world simultaneously.
> —Tamsin E. Lorraine, *Gender, Identity, and the Production of Meaning* (12)

> "What beautiful hyacinths! I have just learnt to love a hyacinth."
> —Catherine Morland, *Northanger Abbey* (174)

Oppositions, such as outsider/insider, male/female, and culture/nature, play an important role in looking at landscape, both the real physical location and the artistic landscape. I do not regard these pairs as necessarily essentialist (in that there is no place in between) or even as hierarchical (although generally in patriarchal western society, "culture" and "male" have been considered superior terms). I regard these oppositions as the ends of continuums along which authors may decide to place their characters, even move characters, or show characters choosing several options during the course of the narrative. Even the exact physical location may be framed, as with a Claude glass, or the artistic landscape may be reinvented in any number of ways, according to the authors' desires. To remain an "outsider," a person views landscape in the culturally prescribed way. I use these oppositions, even though sometimes a character, especially a woman, may feel both within the landscape and yet outside it, a confusing place to be for certain, but nonetheless one suggesting a number of options for her. In other words, she might move along the continuum more freely than if she were confined to either end. This movement along the continuum, remaining on the margin or trying to occupy two places at once, involves the kind of mediation Raymond Williams describes as "a positive process in social reality" (98-99). As we study views of self, linked with views of the world, in this chapter, we will use a combination of Appleton's prospect/refuge theory and Cosgrove's ideas about landscape and social formation.

Cosgrove writes:

> Cultural products like literature, painting, poetry and drama—and landscape—and the aesthetic and moral values with which these are concerned, become mere outgrowths of material productive activity, to be understood by direct reference to the mode of production which happens to dominate the society in which it is produced. (*Landscape* 55-56).

Given this notion of landscape as commodity, the prospect-viewer, in the eighteenth century, traditionally male and gentry, assumed the role of outsider, the landscape becoming all he surveyed. Women did not traditionally have this opportunity to "survey" the landscape, unless, they, like Jane Austen, did it in literature. Women were, indeed, insiders—part of the landscape, what made it picturesque or beautiful. As well, if women were to nature as men to culture, as Sherry Ortner asserts in her article on the subject, they also act as the bridge for bringing the next generation from nature to culture—or from a position of insider (a place women have for many years felt that they must occupy) to a position of cultured male prospect-viewer—outsider. Ortner explains, "Since it is always culture's project to subsume and transcend nature, if women were considered part of nature, then culture would find it 'natural' to subordinate, not to say oppress, them" (73).[1] The way I picture nature/culture and insider/outsider as part of a continuum for the women in Austen's fiction leads me to subscribe to the kind of cultural duality Deborah Kaplan describes in *Jane Austen among Women*. She writes that "Austen may have resorted to indeterminacy as a conscious strategy to avoid having to choose to align in the juvenilia with one *or* the other of her cultures" (12) and Austen "tempered expressions of her women's culture and her dual alliances in works offered to the general public" (13). So Austen uses all the options she can for herself as a writer as well as for her female characters, those of the gentry's culture and those of "women's culture," both of which end up being outsider/insider strategies regarding relationship to the landscape.

***

Exposure. A condition of refuge-deficiency in which the dominant symbolism is that of prospect and hazard combined.
—Appleton, *The Experience of the Landscape* (268)

When Anne Elliot finds herself in a landscape of exposure, as she does on the Cobb at Lyme Regis, she recognizes the open, dangerous nature of the windswept rock seawall for what it is. It is landscape to be appreciated and enjoyed but also to be respected as a potential threat to the viewer's safety. She already knows these things about the landscape and does not need a lesson to help her realize the dangers lurking in what Appleton calls a "locomotion hazard"—"an incident hazard resulting from movement by the threatened party" (269). The "nakedness" of such a prospect-dominant refuge and the total absence, in such a hazard, of any symbols of refuge, although not apparent to the naïve Louisa Musgrove, comes as no surprise to Anne, who immediately takes control of the situation to help the fallen Louisa.

How does this scene, seen through the lens of an aesthetic geographer, relate to the landscapes of the first three novels that Jane Austen wrote? Jane Austen's last novel concerns a heroine who recognizes the safety of the hedgerow and the danger of the Cobb. She does not need to learn from them; she only needs to know them for

---

[1] I use Ortner's definition of culture here: human consciousness by which "humanity attempts to assert control over nature" (72). Ortner believes women are not equivalent to nature but merely considered "closer." Women are "doomed" to mere reproduction, and men "assert creativity externally, 'artificially,' through the medium of technology and symbols" (75). Woman then "accepts her own devaluation and takes culture's point of view" (76).

what they are. In *Northanger Abbey*, *Sense and Sensibility*, and *Pride and Prejudice*, the heroines *do* need to learn from the landscape, and sometimes the landscape they learn from is not located in the "zone of safety." Catherine, Marianne, and Elizabeth find themselves in exposed landscapes where they learn to survive. Their newly discovered knowledge begins to transform them into the kind of women they strive to become from the start—women who have begun to trust their own beliefs about the world and themselves. As philosopher Tamsin Lorraine states, regarding gender identity, "How we see ourselves will be ... linked with how we see the world" (12). So the act of experiencing the landscape is a double one: helping the heroine—or, in this case, heroine-in-training—to interpret the world and to know her own "self," transforming both world and self.

Early in the first chapter of *Northanger Abbey*, the narrator describes Catherine Morland as "in training for a heroine" (11). Marianne appears also to be a heroine-in-training, and Elizabeth, perhaps a little farther along in her "education," still has much to learn. In this chapter, we will examine the landscapes of exposure and knowledge in these first three novels and how and what these three heroines learn. We will continue to use Appleton's theory of prospect and refuge in relation to an artistic, verbal framing of landscape out of nature.

The choice of Bath for the setting of *Northanger Abbey* works well for a landscape of prospects and few refuges, forcing "our heroine-in-training" to learn what she can—with no place to hide. As is clear in Jane Austen's juvenile pieces, her letters, and her later works, the author (and narrator) is very conscious of geography, not just the facts of location but also the way a place might be "framed" as landscape, usually picturesque. The aesthetic environs of Bath and the approach to Northanger Abbey (and the Abbey itself) are all misread by Catherine, all misinterpreted in the light of narrow artistically stereotypical assumptions. Furthermore, what is particularly interesting about Bath as a setting is the way the picturesque views and the city architecture intermingle. Besides the healing qualities of the baths, the reasons people went to Bath then (as they go there even today) were to enjoy the Royal Crescent and to see the other terraced crescents on the hillsides surrounding the city. However, they could also remove themselves quickly to the areas surrounding the city, with views of still more prospects, such as Beechen Cliff, and on to Clifton and Blaise Castle. All these locations are mentioned in *Northanger Abbey*, and yet many times they are perceived differently by Catherine (and possibly by the reader) than they turn out to be, as the narrator eventually discloses.

An intriguing permeability of boundaries between town and country exists in Bath; first, we cross the busy main road by way of Union Passage, and then we move toward the large expanse of green grass at the Royal Crescent "to breathe the fresh air of better company" (*NA* 35). We can travel from the busy shops on Milsom Street to the numerous footpaths climbing into the rolling hills surrounding Bath. The geography of *Northanger Abbey* resembles a series of circles, the center of which is Bath itself. In Bath, social consideration (and lack of it) mixes with exposure in the landscape. As we move toward the environs around Bath, the road to Blaise Castle and Clifton, and the footpath to Beechen Cliff, the heroine-in-training begins to learn the lesson that exposure to the landscape provides. Another concentric circle places Northanger Abbey in Gloucestershire at the north end and

Catherine's home village of Fullerton in Wiltshire at the southern side of the circumference. In any case, our heroine-in-training experiences a sense of vulnerability, especially in her social relationships, which is played out in an exposed landscape. A large gap exists between what seems to be and what really is, and filling this gap becomes Catherine's job as a heroine-in-training.

One instance of such a situation is the abortive drive to Blaise Castle, initiated early in the novel by John and Isabella Thorpe, along with Catherine's brother James Morland. John over-optimistically thinks they can go all the way to Blaise Castle and back in an afternoon, but he miscalculates the distance, and they basically find themselves out on an aimless drive, not seeing much of anything at all. Her brother says, "We had better go back, Thorpe; it is too late to go on to-day; your sister thinks so as well as I. We have been exactly an hour coming from Pulteney-street, very little more than seven miles; and I suppose, we have at least eight more to go" (88). Twice in one day, Catherine has been deceived by John Thorpe: first, when he implies that the Tilneys are not coming to meet her and second, when he promises her the view of Blaise Castle. They could only begin to face reality—the drive was too long for the time they had available, and Catherine is annoyed to have missed both the Tilneys and Blaise.

Another gap between what seems to be and what is concerns Blaise Castle itself: she thinks Blaise Castle is just the ancient ruin she has been reading about in her "horrid" novels. Yet, in fact, Blaise Castle is a "faux" castle, a folly constructed for a gentleman's garden in 1766.[2] Although Catherine never realizes the truth about Blaise Castle, the readers of Jane Austen's time most likely were aware of its recent origin. Christine Alexander points out that all Catherine's false expectations for Blaise Castle are replicated in her visit to Northanger Abbey. Appleton refers to such instances in landscape as reduplication—two similar symbols reinforcing each other. Alexander also establishes that Humphry Repton's designs for Blaise Castle had been completed shortly before Jane Austen began *Northanger Abbey*, and she likely visited the place during one of her stays in Bath. Repton was interested in picturesque and even sublime views from the drives going to the estate and the mansion itself; however, "the Gothic landscape had been accommodated to human activity and comfort" (Alexander 27), as is the landscape of Northanger Abbey.

The gap in Catherine's further education as a heroine-in-training, reading the landscape, must remain incomplete until she visits Northanger Abbey itself and its reinforcing duplication as another kind of "false" Gothic edifice. For Catherine, this gap can only be filled by learning both prescribed "masterly" Gilpinesque ways of reading the landscape and learning to trust her own eyes. Alexander comments on how "Repton valued movement in landscape to create different perspectives and how our understanding of a scene is limited if our view is restricted by a fixed lens or frame" (28). As Catherine grows in her understanding, she chooses many ways of viewing the landscape, from the fixed Claude glass vantage point of Gilpin (as interpreted by Henry Tilney) to the Gothic perspective of Mrs. Radcliffe and finally

---

[2] For more on the history of Blaise Castle and its connections with Humphry Repton and Jane Austen, see Christine Alexander's "The Prospect of Blaise: Landscape and Perception in *Northanger Abbey*" pp. 17-31 (*Persuasions* no. 21, 1999).

one of her own. Catherine must negotiate a position that allows her both to view the landscape as an outsider, yet to relate successfully to it as an insider, a woman with her own personal relationship to it. Here I mean that her success in understanding where she is involves a knowledge of accepted cultural standards (in this case, those of the prospect-viewer) and also the ability to remain at ease within a landscape as she had as a child, when Catherine "hated confinement and cleanliness and loved nothing so well in the world as rolling down the green slope at the back of the house" (10). She had not yet gotten into "training for a heroine."

Social consideration predominates in Catherine's mind when her next opportunity to venture outside Bath occurs. This time, she at least has learned how to say no to the Thorpes' proposal of a trip to Clifton. She chooses instead to walk with Henry and Eleanor Tilney. "They determined on walking round Beechen Cliff, that noble hill whose beautiful verdure and hanging coppice render it so striking an object from almost every opening in Bath" (*N A* 106). This scene contains all the ingredients of real prospect/refuge landscape. Catherine comments on the view, saying she can never see it "without thinking of the south of France" (106). As she uses her Gothic lens to view the scene, Catherine takes considerable imaginative license in viewing the area around Bath as reminiscent of the south of France. She, no doubt, is remembering the setting of *The Mysteries of Udolpho*. (Neither Anne Radcliffe nor the fictional Catherine had ever been to France.) After honestly admitting her ignorance of the principles of landscape art, Catherine receives a "lecture on the picturesque" from Henry Tilney. Of course, here Jane Austen illustrates the limitations of such strict ways of viewing the landscape when Catherine uses her newfound knowledge to "voluntarily reject the whole city of Bath as unworthy to make part of a landscape" (111). Her newly discovered outsider Claude glass view of the landscape precludes her own personal insider view of it. As Cresswell writes: "Places are active forces in the reproduction of norms—in the definition of appropriate practice" (16). Catherine is still the heroine-in-training, learning to define "appropriate practice" in viewing the landscape and unable to separate her own individual views from the powerful social "norms" of her time, as suggested by landscape viewer John Gilpin. She continues trying to find her own way of seeing, still struggling and not yet succeeding.[3]

In voluntarily rejecting the whole city of Bath, based upon a prescriptive way of viewing the scene, Catherine (and Jane Austen) had the example of Humphry Repton. Jane Austen knew all the "rules" of the conventional picturesque and could both use them to describe a landscape such as Pemberley (which, in many ways, for us today feels almost cinematic in its stately movement through the grounds of the estate to the house itself) and, in this case, Bath. Yet she knew very well how to mock the rule-bound scene, as she did when Catherine Morland rejected the view of Bath. (As was shown earlier, Jane Austen, who really admired Gilpin, could still make fun of the stereotypical setting in the fictional piece of her teenaged years,

---

[3] Cosgrove in *Social Formation and Symbolic Landscape* (Totowa, NJ: Barnes and Noble, 1984) asserts that "Bath represents the country house urbanised rather than any expression of a truly classical urban concept" (216). As preconceived notions of the picturesque set Catherine's mind up to reject Bath, so preconceived notions of the Gothic set her up to accept Northanger Abbey before she even arrives there, only to be confused when the estate turns out not to fulfill those notions.

Figure 4.1 Humphry Repton, "Mr. Repton's Opinion of the Aspects," *Red Book Ferne Hall.* **Courtesy of Pierpont Morgan Library, New York. Gift of Mr. Junius S. Morgan and Mr. Henry Morgan, 1954.17. Photography: Joseph Zehavi.**

"Evelyn.") Austen could both use and break the rules, rules that seemed to favor the proprietary landscape viewers, the clients of someone like Humphry Repton.

Many people have seen Repton's "before and after" scenes in his famous Redbooks, but his "Hints for the Improvement of Ferne Hall" from the Redbook even more succinctly state his confident use of a model, drawn as an octagon within a circle, labeled "Mr. Repton's Opinion of Aspects." The views vary from "good" to "not bad," "bad," and "worst" for the north, south, east, and west views from the house. This model reflects the ways in which highly opinionated masculine landowners of the day could label a view, and Repton feels free to make the assumption that anyone would agree with this assessment of the views from the estate. We now know that the "gentlemen's agreement" concerning the lay of the land excluded most women and certainly the heroines of Austen's novels. These heroines actually might have been figures in such set landscapes. Catherine, in a sense, is trying to take up the view of the landscape, defined by Gilpin and Repton and adopted by the "proper" eighteenth-century male proprietors, but she finds that trying to acquiesce to the dominant view so completely and unquestioningly does not really work for her.

As we move away from Bath outward to the larger concentric circle in the geography of *Northanger Abbey*, we can envision another geographical model. This larger circle inscribes the trip to Gloucestershire and to Northanger Abbey itself, followed by a hurried trip seventy miles south to Catherine's Wiltshire home of Fullerton. Bath, it may be noted, lies about halfway between the two. As Catherine arrives at Northanger Abbey, the gap between what she expects and what she actually sees distresses her:

> As they drew near the end of their journey, her impatience for a sight of the abbey—for some time suspended by the conversation on subjects very different—returned in full force, and every bend in the road was expected with solemn awe to afford a glimpse of its massy walls of grey stone, rising amidst a grove of ancient oaks, with the last beams of the sun playing in beautiful splendour on its high gothic windows, but so low did the building stand, that she found herself passing through the great gates of the lodge into the very grounds of Northanger, without having discerned even an antique chimney. (161)

This landscape provides nothing in the way of a Reptonian approach, and "the thick, mizzling rain" (161) obscures any prospect view she might have had. Catherine is disappointed "to pass between lodges of a modern appearance" (161), "the smooth, level road of fine gravel" (161), and the large, clear glass windows, instead of the anticipated "painted glass, dirt, and cobwebs" (161). Catherine finds herself in that gap between expectations and reality with the storm and darkness preventing her from experiencing any real zone of safety in the landscape, neither prospect nor refuge. The landscape is one of exposure.

She begins to learn gradually what the landscape looks like in the daylight from three sources—General Tilney (who turns out to be a surprisingly reliable guide to the scene), Henry Tilney and his sister Eleanor. Although Catherine has some difficulty relinquishing her Gothic perspective of the landscape, she gradually admits that what she anticipated is not what she actually sees. Northanger Abbey's modernization somehow disappoints her expectations, but in Henry's modest parsonage in Woodston she recognizes a place representing the prospect/refuge qualities that will provide a location in which she might flourish.

"What a beautiful hyacinth! I have just learned to love a hyacinth" (174), Catherine tells Henry the morning after experiencing all the imaginative terror of a truly Gothic storm. In one of the few scenes where Jane Austen names a flower, we discover the education from the environment that the author favors.[4] In this conversation with Henry, we find that Catherine cannot tell if the love of hyacinths comes by "accident or argument." When Henry tells her that her love of flowers is "good for her" because it will cause her to go outdoors more, she dismisses this claim by saying that "the pleasure of walking and breathing fresh air is enough for me" (145). Henry persists by saying that "the mere habit of learning to love is the thing; and a teachableness of disposition in a young lady is a great blessing" (145). Henry stays on the side of culture here, while Catherine finds herself between the "accident"—nature and "argument"—culture. This moment seems to be the one where Catherine's learning curve rises sharply; the act of experiencing the hyacinth (object) and interpreting it and her *self* are "inextricably linked."

The "teachableness" proceeds from the landscape itself, not from Henry, although Catherine persists in wishing Henry were there because "now she should not know what was picturesque when she saw it" (177). As the general shows her the grounds of Northanger Abbey in the daylight, she is impressed by its sheltered appearance: "the remainder shut off by knolls of old trees, or luxuriant plantations, and the steep woody hills rising behind, to give it shelter" (177). She judges the scene, relying on her own response alone "without waiting for any better authority" (177). Catherine begins to break away from General Tilney's oppressive authority as she takes the favorite walk of Eleanor's mother, "a narrow winding path through a thick grove of old Scotch firs" (179). She cannot "be kept from stepping forward" (179). Although Catherine persists in her suspicions that General Tilney murdered his wife, her reading of his character as a cold and calculating person remains correct. She now needs some personal experience to back it up, rather than the Gothic conventions that she has substituted for personal knowledge. This personal experience comes from one more landscape of exposure, the seventy-mile, unaccompanied trip home, contrasted with two landscapes of refuge, Woodston, Henry Tilney's home, and Fullerton, Catherine's childhood home, which brings her journey back to its start—full circle, so to speak.

By the time Catherine visits Woodston, Henry's home, some twenty miles from Northanger Abbey, she is only slightly "ashamed to say how pretty she thought it" (212), ignoring the general's criticism of that landscape. Clearly the parsonage and its grounds represent a refuge scene, which in some ways duplicates the landscape of Catherine's home village, Fullerton, containing her father's parsonage, a garden and orchard. The cottage-by-the-wood scene illustrates the refuge value of the landscape at Woodston. As Catherine expresses her delight with the view from a "prettily shaped" sitting room with "windows reaching to the ground" (213), she notices the view.

---

[4] Besides the hyacinth mentioned in *Northanger Abbey*, honeysuckle is mentioned in *Sense and Sensibility*, "As a house, Barton Cottage, though small, was comfortable and compact; but as a cottage it was defective, for the building was regular, the roof was tiled, and the window shutters were not painted green, nor were the walls covered with honeysuckle" (28). This was the new home of the Dashwood sisters after their old home was taken over by their brother. Austen is poking fun at the stereotypical image the Dashwoods had of a honeysuckle-covered, thatched-roof cottage—not a "real" cottage but a faux cottage out of the middle-class English imagination.

"Oh! What a sweet little cottage there is among the trees—apple trees, too! It is the prettiest cottage!"
"You like it—you approve it as an object—it is enough. Henry, remember that Robinson is spoken to about it. The cottage remains." (214)

This is General Tilney's reply to Catherine before he realizes she is not the rich heiress he had assumed she was; however, we as readers can imagine the Reptonian conversation concerning "improvements" and the possible removal of the little "eyesore" of a cottage from the view of the parsonage.[5]

Before Catherine arrives at her family home, a duplication of a similar kind of refuge she recognized at Woodston, she finds herself in a duplication of the exposure scene she experienced on the road to Blaise Castle. That scene exposes Catherine to social indiscretion (as she rides in a carriage with a single man unchaperoned), and her stay at Northanger Abbey exposes her to social humiliation and the actual social cruelty of General Tilney. Being turned out into a real hazardous situation, the forced journey alone seventy miles to her home, becomes one of the greatest lessons she learns from the landscape.

Early nineteenth-century readers would surely recognize the very real cruelty of General Tilney in turning out a seventeen year old girl to find her way home with no money or escort. Although the general may not have tortured or murdered his wife in true Gothic style, he is certainly breaking the cultural laws of which Henry has already reminded Catherine when she confesses her suspicions to him: "Remember the country and the age in which we live. Remember that we are English, that we are Christians. Consult your own understanding, your own sense of the probable, your own observations of what is passing around you" (196). Now Catherine sees that she really was not far from the mark in her earlier assessment of General Tilney.

Jane Austen's awareness of geography makes us even more sensitive to General Tilney's ruthless disregard of Catherine's safety. Catherine has been taken to Northanger Abbey, far to the north of Bath in Gloucestershire, and now must find her way home to Fullerton in Wiltshire, near Salisbury, almost as far south of Bath. But Catherine has learned to trust her own assessment of the landscape. She no longer fears the Gothic elements of Northanger Abbey. She is able to lie awake during her last night there "without curiosity or terror" (227). Catherine has learned to question the value and meaning of space. Again, "the effect of place is not simply a geographical matter. It always intersects with sociocultural expectations" (Cresswell 8). Now that Catherine knows where she really stands (both literally and figuratively), she begins to reassess it on her own "by the review of objects on which she had first looked under impressions so different" (230).

Although this trip is instigated by the general's total lack of social concern for Catherine, "the journey itself held no terrors for her" (230), and she manages to deal with it successfully all alone. So although the narrator describes Catherine's

---

[5] Interestingly enough, reduplication occurs with Blaise Castle not being what it seemed as well. It should be noted that Repton's Redbook of Blaise calls for a cottage to be visible from the castle. While not visible from Northanger Abbey (also not what it seemed to Catherine), the view of the cottage from the parsonage at Woodston follows closely on the description of the Abbey grounds.

entrance to her village as a "humiliation of her biographer to relate" (233), yet we readers can recognize her trip home as Catherine's real understanding of how to relate to the landscape as it really is for her. The narrator of this novel describes Catherine, even as a child, as a self-sufficient person and one who welcomes a chance to be outdoors. Unsurprisingly, she maintains her composure both on a solo journey through the landscape and after her less than triumphant return home. But this heroine-in-training brings with her some additional knowledge. Catherine's experience in *Northanger Abbey* "questions the naturalness and absoluteness of assumed geographies" (Cresswell 149)—and landscapes as well. No more will she assume a landscape she sees as one from a novel or a city view as unworthy because it does not exactly meet the rules of Gilpinese framing. She can now rely on her own experience in the landscape and use it to her advantage. She has had an education in how one might view the landscape and the real experience in viewing it. Now she is ready to interpret the landscape through her own personal lens and decide whether she herself wants to "learn to love a hyacinth."

A "model" for the kind of gaze associated with Jane Austen—both her narratorial gaze and the gaze she allows her female characters—we find in a watercolor by Samuel Palmer called "View from Rook's Hill, Kent," (c. 1843). Yes, it was painted around twenty-five years after Jane Austen's death, but, it is both a way of picturing Catherine Morland seeing Bath without Henry Tilney's aesthetic "help" and also a way other Jane Austen heroines might have learned from their landscape, as they hid on the edge of it and sought knowledge without exposure. There is artifice here, yet, as Appleton suggests, using the symbolism of the environment frees the viewer from its tyranny. The three women with their dog grouped together on the side of a clearing on Rook's Hill have an ideal zone of safety, protective coloration, so to speak, and a view of the rolling countryside below them. They can both hide and seek; the viewer of this painting does not feel like a voyeur on the scene but someone who might feel welcome to join them in the view. A woman does not have to "learn to love a hyacinth" and "voluntarily reject the whole city of Bath." She has other options. By blending in with the landscape as she looks out upon another landscape, she finds she can actually learn more, if she finds the right prospect and the right refuge.

***

In a natural economy the relationship between human beings and land is predominantly that of the insider, an unalienated relationship based on use values and interpreted analogically. In a capitalist economy it is a relationship between owner and commodity, an alienated relationship wherein man stands as outsider and interprets nature causally ... The idea of landscape holds both types of relationship in an unstable unity.
— Cosgrove, *Social Formation and Symbolic Landscape* (64)

"I am convinced," said Edward, "that you really feel all the delight in a fine prospect which you profess to feel. But, in return, your sister must allow me to feel no more than I profess. I like a fine prospect, but not on picturesque principles. I do not like crooked, twisted, blasted trees. I admire them much more if they are tall, straight and flourishing. I do not like ruined, tattered cottages. I am not fond of nettles, or thistles, or heath blossoms.

Figure 4.2 Samuel Palmer. "View from Rook's Hill, Kent" (1843). Courtesy of Yale Center for British Art. Paul Mellon Collection.

I have more pleasure in a snug farm-house than a watch-tower—and a troop of tidy, happy villagers please me better than the finest banditti in the world."

(*Sense and Sensibility* 97-98)

As we examine the ways landscape can be seen in *Sense and Sensibility*, the separation between those characters who observe the landscape as reasoning outsiders, seeing it as a commodity, and those who move into the landscape and experience nature in its totality becomes quickly apparent. Although Marianne may be perceived at first as very much the experiencer, like her fellow heroine-in-training, Catherine, she learns to trust her experience in landscapes of exposure while learning to respect and understand the more practical view of Edward and Colonel Brandon. Denis Cosgrove's insights into landscape formation express how unstable the outsider (proprietor/owner) view of the landscape is when expressed in literature with the insider (experiential) view. In *Sense and Sensibility*, we find characters ranging from John Dashwood, who turns all aspects of landscape into financial gains, to Marianne, who, like Wordsworth's Lucy, comes dangerously close to "death by landscape," yet survives, maintaining her intimacy with the landscape while acknowledging the value of landscape as commodity. In *Sense and Sensibility*, Jane Austen successfully manages to maintain both views of the landscape: to portray a female character that can fully respond to nature and yet maintain a place in society, confining though that may be.

In *Sense and Sensibility*, we see landscapes of refuge and landscapes of exposure, both of which affect the experiential learning of the young heroine-in-training, in this case, Marianne Dashwood. Marianne experiences the land in ways that language cannot express. Unlike the less complicated, more docile Catherine, Marianne rejects the fashionable language of landscape common in books such as *The Tourist's Grammar*:[6]

"It is very true," said Marianne, "that admiration of landscape scenery is become a mere jargon. Every body pretends to feel and tries to describe with the taste and elegance of him who first defined what picturesque beauty was. I detest jargon of every kind, and sometimes I have kept my feelings to myself, because I could not find any language to describe them in but what was worn and hackneyed out of all sense and meaning." (97)

Cosgrove might describe Marianne's early experience in the landscape as "the unreflexive subjectivism of the insider where the feeling for the land is incommunicable through the artificial language of art" (64). And indeed, when Marianne does try to express herself concerning her old home, she sounds stilted, "And you, ye well-known trees!—but you will continue the same.—No leaf will

---

[6] *The Tourist's Grammar on Rules Relating to the Scenery and Antiquities Incident to Traveller: compiled from the first authorities, and including An Epitome of Gilpin's Principles of the Picturesque* was published in 1826; however, it is typical of the kind of guide to viewing the landscape with which Jane Austen was familiar. In *The Tourist's Grammar*, the Reverent T. Fosbroke gives such instructions as these: "*Copses* are not picturesque. They have not the projections and recesses which the skirts of forests exhibit. The best effect of them is on the lofty banks of a river. Viewed upwards, the deficiencies are concealed" (xii). With such a guide, it is no wonder Catherine dismissed all of Bath as lacking the proper landscape attributes.

decay because we are removed" (27). It is difficult for someone who feels the landscape so deeply to express it in words. Because nature is associated with the feminine, a woman may find it easier to be *in* and *of* the landscape than to stand back and analyze it—if she goes along with social norms—what is "only natural"—a phrase we will explore more deeply in *Emma*.

If we then associate men with the proprietor/owner of the landscape, we find most of the male characters in both *Northanger Abbey* and *Sense and Sensibility* identify with that role. Obviously men like General Tilney control the estates, such as Northanger Abbey. And even if Henry Tilney does not control the estate, yet he has the language of landscape under control and tries to teach it to Catherine. Far over on the controller continuum in *Sense and Sensibility* is the mercenary John Dashwood, who describes Norland to Elinor entirely in terms of financial gains and losses. "The inclosure of Norland Common, now carrying on, is a most serious drain" (225). He describes the removal of a stand of old walnut trees (at a profit) and the erection of a greenhouse on the hill in its place.

Yet other male characters as well take this seemingly practical view toward the landscape. Edward Ferrars, although he does not own property, manages to stand apart from the landscape and see it more "objectively" or, at least, with less emotion than does Marianne, much to her irritation. He likes "tall, straight, flourishing" trees, presumably trees which have more financial value. He likes a "snug farm house" and "tidy, happy villagers," signs of affluence appreciated by any aspiring capitalist. Even Colonel Brandon's ownership of Delaford, "a nice old fashioned place, full of comfort and conveniences" (196), puts Brandon in a position of power to help Edward. Willoughby too knows he must look at the landscape in terms of financial gain, much as he has allowed Marianne to believe that he sees the landscape as she does. The proprietary landscape is that which both Cosgrove and Cresswell remark in their research in aesthetic geography allocates space to control people and things.

However, Marianne's experiential relationship to the landscape eventually encompasses at least enough understanding of the value of ownership to ensure her survival when she manages to endure exposure in a landscape that seems all prospect, no refuge. This was the landscape that, at first, gives her the feeling of "all the happy privilege ... of wandering from place to place in free and luxurious solitude" (303). However, she has the same disregard of the dangers of exposure that later Louisa Musgrove exhibits in *Persuasion*. Her reflection on the danger of emotions experienced in an exposed landscape, coupled with the eventual knowledge of the economic reasons for Willoughby's desertion, assists her in understanding her other ways of seeing the landscape.

Going back to prospect/refuge theory of aesthetic geography and applying it here, we can see that when the Dashwood family leaves the refuge-dominant location of Norland for Barton Cottage, they have again found a zone of safety as well as a zone of contact.

> The situation of the house was good. High hills rose immediately behind, and at no great distance on each side; some of which were open downs, the others cultivated and woody. The village of Barton was chiefly on one of these hills, and formed a pleasant view from the cottage windows. The prospect in front was more extensive; it commanded the whole

of the valley, and reached into the country beyond. The hills which surrounded the cottage terminated the valley in that direction. ... (28-29)

From this description, the cottage (only "defective" in that it is "regular") has prospects, provides refuge, and remains close to Barton Park, yet "screened from their view at home by the projection of an hill" (32). All these aspects of the cottage indicate a safe place, the "screen" even acting as a coulisse, sometimes defined as a piece of scenery projecting from the wings of a stage set. In landscape, a coulisse provides "a particular form of interface between voids and masses, highly significant as a zone of contact between prospect and refuge" (Appleton 268). The landscape then provides some privacy from the outside world for the women. (We will see later that Elinor provides other protective "screens," both painted and social.) As a zone of contact, the area near the cottage acts as an interface between the refuge-dominant scene of the cottage and the prospect-dominant scene of the hills and downs of the general area.

Just as Catherine learns to act as an independent thinker and feeler as a result of her interaction with landscapes of exposure, so does Marianne, initially stumbling on the downs and meeting Willoughby, and then experiencing a duplication of the scene as she wanders in the exposed hills around Cleveland. In a striking early scene at Barton, Marianne and her younger sister Margaret see the landscape of exposure near their home.

> The whole country about them abounded in beautiful walks. The high downs which invited them from almost every window of the cottage to seek the exquisite enjoyment of air on their summits, were an happy alternative when the dirt of the valleys beneath shut up their superior beauties; and towards one of these hills did Marianne and Margaret one memorable morning direct their steps, attracted by the partial sunshine of a showery sky, and unable longer to bear the confinement. (40-41)

The high downs here are considered "falling ground," "a surface sloping downwards away from a vantage-point; a common prospect symbol" (Appleton 268). The whole scene is one of exposure. No refuge, yet prospect and hazard remain in combination. The scene involves the meteorological hazard of rain (which occurs later at Cleveland as well), the rain and the slope contributing to Marianne twisting her foot and being "rescued" by the stranger, Willoughby. Marianne's exposure to Willoughby is both physical and emotional. The emotional aspect continues long after her twisted ankle heals, leading her, unrealistically, to emphasize the romantic qualities of exposed landscapes (and feelings). Marianne continues to expose herself, even visiting the estate of Willoughby's elderly cousin alone with Willoughby. She explains the lack of propriety to Elinor by saying, "If there had been any real impropriety in what I did, I should have been sensible of it at the time, for we always know when we are acting wrong, and with such a conviction I could have had no pleasure" (68). Elinor replies that Marianne has "exposed" herself to many "impertinent remarks," but Marianne is not ready to learn from the landscape of exposure yet.

Much of this novel is set in London, but unlike the Bath of *Northanger Abbey*, with its natural settings interspersed with street scenes, the London scenes are social hothouses with no places to seek refuge and few prospects. Hanging over Mrs.

Jennings' mantelpiece is the only available landscape, one of "coloured silks" (160) by Charlotte Palmer, the least reflective and probably the most shallow character in the novel. Instead of the skies of landscapes above the fireplace, "real "weather" exists in the country far away and only affects Marianne in delaying the sportsmen's (and presumably Willoughby's) appearance in the city. Significantly, one interesting reference to aesthetic geography that does appear in some of the London scenes is the use of screens. Screens in the natural landscape are similar to the coulisses, wings on stage scenery, which act as interfaces between refuge and prospect or partial blocks of vistas. In the London scenes, Elinor provides the screens. Tony Tanner, in his introduction to *Sense and Sensibility*, discusses Elinor and Marianne in terms of screens: "Jane Austen has brought us to the point of feeling some positive approbation and appreciation for both the maintainer of screens [Elinor] and the discarder of screens [Marianne]" (17).

Before they even go to London, attempting to protect Marianne from disappointment, Elinor tries to "screen" her from approaching someone she mistakes for Willoughby. Again, Elinor tries to "screen" Marianne "from the observation of others" (177), following the upsetting encounter with Willoughby at the ball. In a way Elinor herself is acting like a coulisse, providing cover for Marianne so that other people cannot know her feelings and leave her exposed. Elinor paints screens as well and has given a pair of them to her sister-in-law. The screens are praised by guests at her home but slighted by Mrs. Ferrars, who fears Elinor's influence on her son Edward. (Miss Morton, the family's choice for Edward, is praised for painting a beautiful landscape.) Elinor is not as effective in maintaining her screening of Marianne's feelings as she is in screening her own feelings from others; nevertheless, she persists in acting as a screen in the landscape.

In another landscape of exposure, Marianne refuses to screen her emotions altogether and exposes herself entirely to the hazards of landscape at the Palmers' estate, Cleveland. She immediately leaves the house:

> stealing away through the winding shrubberies, now just beginning to be in beauty to gain a distant eminence; where, from its Grecian temple, her eye, wandering over a wide tract of country to the south-east, could fondly rest on the farthest ridge of hills in the horizon, and fancy that from their summits Combe Magna [Willoughby's estate] might be seen. (303-303)

This landscape becomes not a zone of safety for Marianne so much as a prospect-heavy landscape of exposure. The Grecian temple (another romantic image) places her high on a hill, to accept the full emotional impact of the scene. In "moments of precious, invaluable misery, she rejoiced in tears of agony" (303), definitely allowing her emotions to be heightened by the landscape of exposure. Of course, we know that several such walks about the grounds in damp air lead to what the apothecary describes as Marianne's "putrid tendency."

Unlike the unfortunate Sophia in "Love and Freindship," Marianne narrowly escapes "death by landscape." And that which does not kill her makes her stronger. A final reduplication of the landscape of exposure, "the full view of the hill, the important hill behind" (344), where Marianne first met Willoughby illustrates what she has learned. During this scene, Elinor removes the final screen she has placed to protect Marianne and her feelings, relating Willoughby's explanation for his previous behavior to her. Marianne then begins to understand that total insider exposure to the landscape (in this case, voluntary) equates to attempted suicide: "Had I died,—it would have been self-destruction. I did not know my danger till the danger was removed; but with such feelings as these reflections gave me, I wonder at my recovery" (346). She is able to experience the memory of her first meeting Willoughby on the hill and yet also to understand why he needs to stay in a proprietary spectator position regarding the landscape. Finally, as a result of being able to understand both ways of experiencing the landscape, she can accept Colonel Brandon and his refuge at Delaford.

A final telling scene shows how constraints might be overcome and how new options for dealing with dilemmas—either in personal or landscape relations—might be handled. Edward explains to Elinor that he is free to marry her. "He rose from his seat and walked to the window, apparently from not knowing what to do; took up a pair of scissars [sic] that lay there, and while spoiling both them and their sheath by cutting the latter to pieces as he spoke," told her about his release from his engagement to Lucy Steele (360). Perhaps this image is one of release from the constraints of an either/or situation, allowing both sense and sensibility to coexist in the landscape together.

***

> The great advantage of the writer is that, since his landscape pictures have to be coded into words and then decoded by the reader into pictures, there are two opportunities for the enrichment of the landscape by the imagination.
> —Appleton, *The Experience of the Landscape* (214)

> At once ambiguous, attractive, and important, the visible landscape reflects the human values and ideologies of the resident and viewer, serving as a palimpsest of place attachments between individuals and social groups to specific locations and places.
> —Greg Ringer, *Cultural Landscapes of Tourism* (7)

> [A]t that moment she felt, that to be mistress of Pemberley might be something!
> —Elizabeth Bennet, *Pride and Prejudice* (267)

The center of the novel *Pride and Prejudice* contains one of the greatest landscape scenes in English literature, one that has been commented upon extensively since its publication nearly 200 years ago. Here we will look at this scene from yet another perspective, regarding it as the "final examination" for the heroine-in-training, Elizabeth Bennett, an examination that she passes with flying colors. If we return to the passages quoted earlier in this chapter by Lorraine and Cosgrove, we can better judge the success of the Pemberley chapters in *Pride and Prejudice*. Lorraine refers to "creations of an activity that constitutes self and world simultaneously" (12), and that is what happens when Elizabeth first sees Pemberley. She finally learns who she can be and what the world can be; at the same time, she has "passed" the final test in understanding who Darcy really is as she walks through the house and around the grounds at Pemberley. Roger Sales describes the experience of Pemberley as something much more than showing off.

Yet its appeal is not an aesthetic feast for the eye so much as it is an expression of its owner. Without being in any worked-out way symbolic, wood, stream, hill, and house here are all Darcy; the whole may seem remote and aloof, but Elizabeth can sense it is not so really, though it is indeed proud. It is a mistake to conclude that Elizabeth thinks it would be "something" to be Pemberley's mistress as a matter of ownership; obviously what she is responding to is the estate as the expression of Darcy. (41)

As we continue to gaze at the landscape of *Pride and Prejudice*, we will observe other outdoors scenes where Elizabeth, our final heroine-in-training, moves toward a continuous expansion of her knowledge of the world and herself, each changing the other.

But before moving to other scenes, we need to examine features that make the Pemberley passages of *Pride and Prejudice* work so well. We might recall that Cosgrove in *Social Formation and Symbolic Landscape* discusses "the ambiguity in landscape between individual and social meaning" (64) and the difficulty in reconciling the "unalienated" insider, analogic relationship with landscape, and the "alienated" outsider relationship of owner and commodity. The Pemberley section deals successfully with both these issues.

First, let us deal with analogy and the personal individual relationship to the landscape. Jane Austen clearly means to show us, as Sales states, that Pemberley basically *is* Darcy. Elizabeth knows early in the novel that Darcy owns one of the largest estates in the country, so when she sees it, she should not be surprised at its grandeur. However, every feature of the estate represents Darcy's character. Pemberley House itself is "a large, handsome, stone building," the stream is one of "some natural importance" but "without artificial appearance," "its banks were neither formal, nor falsely adorned," and Elizabeth "had never seen a place for which nature had done more, or where natural beauty had been so little counteracted by awkward taste" (267). Not only is Jane Austen describing landscape, she is also describing Darcy himself, and Elizabeth recognizes him for what he is immediately by analogy. Compared with Rosings (and Darcy's aunt herself, also by analogy), there is "less of splendor, and more real elegance" (246). Her recognition of Darcy's true self in Pemberley places Elizabeth in the position of unalienated insider in the landscape. Even the thought of it causes her to blush as she recognizes how intimate such a position might be for her.

But Pemberley is big enough to encompass the socially exclusive relationship of owner and commodity as well, and initially there might be some question whether Elizabeth can ever "belong" in such a place, coming from such an economically and socially inferior background. She just begins to understand the personal significance of Pemberley and what it might have been to her when she realizes its social significance—one of class consciousness: "My uncle and aunt would have been lost to me: I should not have been allowed to invite them" (246). How this analogic aspect of the Pemberley chapters and the class-conscious relationship are reconciled finally allows Elizabeth to know her "self" and the "object"—Pemberley/Darcy more completely. Jane Austen had never been a snob about social/economic class; however, as is pointed out by Tristram in "Jane Austen and the Changing Face of England," Austen's focus on people of "low money" becomes greater in *Pride and Prejudice*. The problem, and the character flaw to be laughed at, is pretending to be someone a person is not.[7] Elizabeth's aunt and uncle never try to hide the sources of their money or their true social status. Elizabeth learns from her visit to Pemberley that Darcy can easily welcome, as part of his social set, members of a "lower" class. His speedy and gracious invitation to Mr. Gardiner to join him in fishing the streams at Pemberley and subsequent invitations to the Gardiners to dine at Pemberley indicate that Darcy does not feel he is demeaning himself by entertaining Elizabeth's landless relations. Even though Darcy owns one of the most extensive estates in England, he respects a man who, openly and honestly, makes his living in trade. As Darcy himself has said earlier in the novel, "Where there is a real superiority of mind, pride will be always under good regulation" (57). Elizabeth recognizes this regulation of pride in Darcy himself as he welcomes the company of such honest, intelligent middle-class people as the Gardiners.

As Tony Tanner writes in his introduction to *Pride and Prejudice*, "Man, and woman, need to be *both* an experiencer *and* a reasoner ... Both experience and reason depend upon impressions" (13). Like Catherine and Marianne, Elizabeth learns from her interaction with landscape. As Catherine and Marianne, Elizabeth likes being outdoors, especially in what might be termed "landscapes of exposure." Unlike Catherine, she starts out with a fair degree of self-assurance both in her personal experience in the landscape and in her artistic knowledge of it. Unlike Marianne, she does not impose an unrealistically romantic layer on the landscape of exposure. Examining two scenes at Netherfield reveals evidence of this self-assurance. The first involves Elizabeth's trip to Netherfield by foot to nurse her sister.

> Elizabeth continued her walk alone, crossing field after field at a quick pace, jumping over stiles and springing over puddles with impatient activity, and finding herself at last within view of the house, with weary ancles, dirty stockings, and a face glowing with the warmth of exercise. (32)

That Mrs. Hurst and Miss Bingley "held her in contempt for it" (33) and that Darcy becomes even more attracted to her does not seem to affect Elizabeth. Confidence in an exposed landscape Mrs. Hurst and Miss Bingley condemn as "wild" and inappropriate; however, confidence in the open landscape Darcy finds particularly attractive. Elizabeth is oblivious to both the censure and the admiration. Her experience in such open areas gives her confidence in traversing them and will assist her in learning about other less familiar landscapes such as the grounds at Rosings and Pemberley.

While Catherine is still learning to view the landscape as an artist, Elizabeth uses her knowledge of landscape art to her advantage shortly after she arrives at Netherfield in this second scene illustrating her assurance in outdoor settings. Only the threat of the inferiority of her "low connections" (36) is keeping Darcy from courting Elizabeth at this point. Miss Bingley recognizes this attraction, as she walks with him through the shrubbery, taunting him about portraits of Elizabeth's

---

[7] Tristram adds in *Living Space* that Austen's belief in honesty explains why she sometimes satirizes cottages if the owner or admirer sees it as "quaint" or a cottage orneé, such as those admired by Mr. Parker in *Sanditon*.

aunt and uncle to be hung in the gallery at Pemberley next to Darcy's illustrious ancestors. When Elizabeth and Mrs. Hurst arrive at an apparently narrow and sheltered walk, one aesthetically connected with prospect/refuge landscape, the others offer to move to the broader (and more exposed) avenue. Elizabeth quickly declines the offer telling them, "You are charmingly group'd, and appear to uncommon advantage. The picturesque would be spoilt by admitting a fourth" (53). Elizabeth has learned well not only her landscape aesthetics but also her ability to control what appears in the frame and what does not. We might recall Jane Austen's youthful story "Evelyn" and the four cows that she "disposed at equal distances" and the ability the arranger has to laugh at such artificiality. We can be certain that Elizabeth has learned to control this landscape aesthetically, and we are aware of her pleasure in such artistic control as "she then ran gaily off, rejoicing as she rambled about, in the hope of being at home in a day or two" (53).

"When something occurs to offer Elizabeth happiness, independence, love—something we know is good for her, Austen sets it out of doors," claims Lisa Altomari (50). Our heroine-in-training, Elizabeth, learns some of her major lessons concerning self, and her connection to the world as well, in the outdoors, especially while visiting the grounds of Rosings. Elizabeth needs to see Rosings in order to appreciate Pemberley. Rosings has its "beauty and its prospects" but these were the results of "the mere stateliness of money and rank" (161). From her lessons at Rosings, Elizabeth learns to recognize landscape that reflects more than those superficial qualities.

Elizabeth chooses boundary walks, walks that seem to fall into that aesthetic geographical category of zones of safety, sites of both prospect and refuge. Choosing to walk along such boundaries, other heroines in later Austen fiction make interesting discoveries about themselves and others (Fanny near the park palings at Sotherton and Charlotte Heywood along the park palings at Sanditon House). In this case, Elizabeth's "favorite walk, and where she frequently went while the others were calling on Lady Catherine, was along the open grove which edged that side of the park, where there was a nice sheltered path, which no one seemed to value but herself" (169). Here she could remain in touch simultaneously with society and nature—a good place to hide and a good place from which to seek.

Even after Elizabeth has rejected Darcy's proposal (offered indoors), and she wants to avoid him, she still walks along the boundary of the park. It is on this walk that Darcy finds her and hands her the letter explaining his previous actions concerning Wickham and Bingley. In this landscape, she performs a double act of learning. She thinks, "Till this moment, I never knew myself" (208). She needs to be out on this boundary walk to learn not just who Darcy is but who she is. She can now see her family and Longbourne more clearly and separated from herself, seen the way they are by other discerning persons. She can also now see Darcy more clearly, apart from her "first impressions" (Austen's original title for *Pride and Prejudice*) at Meryton and from his associations with Rosings and his overbearing aunt. The landscape at Rosings has prepared Elizabeth well for her visit to Pemberley.

Ringer writes that the landscape "reflects the human values and ideologies of the resident and viewer, serving as a palimpsest of place attachments between individuals and social groups to specific locations and places" (7). By the time

Elizabeth reaches Pemberley, she has the necessary experiences and knowledge of place to recognize the layers of meaning in the landscape. The fields and walks at Netherfield—really the old familiar landscape of her childhood—and the parkland at Rosing—have prepared her for her final test as a heroine-in-training. And we, as readers, have every reason to believe she will pass the test because of her grounding in nature. We know she will remember what she sees and use it when we read her reaction to the planned trip to the Lake District (which becomes instead a trip to Pemberley):

> What are men to rocks and mountains? Oh! What hours of transport we shall spend! And when we do return, it shall not be like other travellers, without being able to give one accurate idea of any thing. We will know where we have gone—we will recollect what we have seen. Lakes, mountains, and rivers shall not be jumbled together in our imaginations; nor, when we attempt to describe any particular scene, will we begin quarrelling about its relative situation. (154)

Although Elizabeth never makes it to the Lake District, her recollections of the scenes she does see stay clearly in her mind. She can carry with her the attachments of one place along to the next. We might imagine that after seeing Pemberley, she and Darcy will not quarrel over their different perceptions of a landscape; they will know what they see.

When Elizabeth eventually returns to Longbourne, she carries with her all her newfound knowledge. No longer a heroine-in-training, she can face off with Lady Catherine in the "prettyish kind of a little wilderness" (352), actually a clump of trees with no real prospect or refuge qualities. Elizabeth wonders how she could have believed that Lady Catherine and her nephew Darcy were alike. Elizabeth is quite comfortable in this landscape, knowing herself and the lay of the land perfectly. Not only does she have an experiential relationship to the land, she knows where she stands socially as well. When Lady Catherine says to her, "If you were sensible of your own good, you would not wish to quit the sphere, in which you have been brought up" (356), Elizabeth can easily reply "I should not consider myself as quitting that sphere. He is a gentleman; I am a gentleman's daughter; so far we are equal" (356). The "sphere" referred to here is both social and geographical. Elizabeth can remember Pemberley as an insider and an outsider regarding the landscape. She has acquired the necessary palimpsest of place attachments between individuals and social groups to particular locations, from Longbourne to Netherfield, from Rosings to Pemberley. These layers of attachments, experience, and knowledge build up in Elizabeth's mind, preparing her for scenes such as this one with Lady Catherine.

Pride and Prejudice ends with a feast of observing the landscape and walking about, with Darcy and Elizabeth wandering about "beyond her own knowledge" (373), which at this point is considerable. Her "graduation" from heroine-in-training to true heroine dates, according to Elizabeth's own admission, to her "first seeing his beautiful grounds at Pemberley" (372). We, the readers, have the great advantage, mentioned by Appleton, of taking the landscape of words and decoding it into pictures, providing for ourselves a heightened ability to enjoy the gaze upon Jane Austen's landscape.

In the next chapter we move from heroines-in-training to heroines like Fanny, from whom others must learn, and Emma, who begins to understand and respect the social power she already has. Fanny and Emma have very different temperaments, but they do have one thing in common. Each "belongs" to a place. Fanny belongs to Mansfield Park; Emma belongs to Highbury. Leaving these "enclaves of civility" for the more threatening places of Portsmouth or Box Hill exposes them to landscapes of "clamorous impertinence." In the end each reaffirms her love of the landscape of her true home.

Chapter 5

Enclaves of Civility amidst Clamorous Impertinence

> The social and the spatial are so thoroughly imbued with each other's presence that their analytical separation quickly becomes a misleading exercise. Indeed, a sustained investigation of the "out of place" metaphor points to the fact that social power and social resistance are always already spatial. When an expression such as "out of place" is used, it is impossible to clearly demarcate whether social or geographical place is denoted—place always means both.
>
> (Cresswell 11)

> Landscape is anchored in *human life*, not something to look at but to live in, and to live in socially. Landscape is a *unity* of people and environment which opposes in its reality the false dichotomy of man and nature.
>
> (Cosgrove 35)

The 1996 Miramax film version of *Emma* opens in outer space, hurling the viewer towards Earth, moving in on Europe, then closer to England, and finally focusing on Highbury, in this case, the purported center of the Universe. With this particular opening, these filmmakers suggest the significant relationship between geography and *Emma*. Highbury *is* the center of the Universe for Emma—and for just about everyone else in the novel. The characters can hardly move outside of it (and its satellite estates) without something unsettling happening to them. In many ways, Mansfield Park shares a similar position in Austen's novel of the same name. Although a large estate, instead of a village aspiring to become a town, Mansfield Park also acts as the center of the Universe for its characters, and characters moving outside its confinements find themselves in a virtual state of exile. They are always brought back, in memory at least, to that center of the Universe, "a description of the people, the manners, the amusements, the ways of Mansfield Park" (419).

Place and the heroine in both *Mansfield Park* (published in 1815) and *Emma* (published in 1816) are inextricably connected. These novels, we know, were both conceived and written by Austen while she lived at Chawton, her home during the last eight years of her life. Both novels deal with heroines who move from zones of safety, Mansfield Park or Hartfield, to landscapes of exposure—exposure not so much to their physical safety but to a questioning of who they themselves are. What is their true sense of self? Using Appleton's aesthetic geographical perspective, we see how the "right" landscape provides a way for each heroine to control her own destiny as well as stare down the prospect of finding herself in a landscape of social exposure, with only her "self" to count on. In *Mansfield Park* and *Emma*, Jane Austen moves from heroines-in-training, Catherine, Marianne, and Elizabeth, who discover a landscape to thrive within, to Fanny Price and Emma Woodhouse, who find their strength in the landscapes of home, Mansfield Park and Highbury and its satellites. These places become, for them, "enclaves of civility amidst clamorous impertinence."[1]

As we observe the communities of Mansfield Park and Highbury, we notice how Austen moves toward the love of looking inward, not so much as a gaze upon the landscape but a position within it. Unlike the gentlemen proprietors in the eighteenth-century landscape pictures, with their outsider view, she is moving the reader toward a heroine who can both reflect on her position inside the landscape and appreciate the unique significance of the social and physical landscape for others. In the case of Mansfield Park, Tony Tanner comments that "Mansfield, as a place, as an institution, can take raw material from Portsmouth, and refine it" (14). Mansfield *is* the enclave of civility; Portsmouth and London are all "clamorous impertinence." Everyone and every place near Highbury seem to "belong to Highbury." As Mr. Woodhouse says, "In London it is always a sickly season" (102). In these "enclaves of civility," Austen emphasizes order, peace, regularity, harmony, and propriety. All else belongs to "clamorous impertinence." Enclaves of civility and clamorous impertinence correspond rather closely with the aesthetic geographic notions of landscapes of safety and those of exposure.

The gaze in these two novels by a woman and the focus upon a female protagonist distinguishes itself from the proprietor's view. As was briefly mentioned before, Gillian Rose discusses such a gaze in *Feminism and Geography: The Limits of Geographical Knowledge*. In this critical work, she particularly focuses upon Gainsborough's "Mr. and Mrs. Andrews" to illustrate woman's relationship to the landscape as depicted by a male artist. Rose describes the woman's role as "naturalized by the references to trees and fields" (93). Rose contends, as well, that "the gaze ... renders her [Mrs. Andrews] as immobile, as natural, as productive and as decorative as the lands" (93). In viewing this painting, Mrs. Andrews appears almost attached to the tree as by some process of graceful symbiosis, while Mr. Andrews stands slightly in front of her and gazes proudly away, seemingly to mark the ownership of his estate. Mrs. Andrews herself, while still alert to her position and prominent in the landscape seems to have no other recourse than to remain "stuck." Although Emma and Fanny may relate to the landscape and feel harmonious with it, neither blends in with it nor becomes part of the landscape in the way Gainsborough's Mrs. Andrews is forced to do. Austen certainly understands thoroughly the traditional position of the "natural" and "decorative" woman in the landscape. We see Mr. Elton praising both Harriet and a tree in the same breath, as he flatters Emma's efforts at painting: "I regard it as a most happy thought, the placing of Miss Smith out of doors; and the tree is touched with such inimitable spirit!" (48). Just as Gainsborough naturalizes Mrs. Andrews and the tree, Mr. Elton sees Harriet the same way, except the tree is the "spirited" object. (We might go back to Austen's juvenile "Evelyn" where Mr. Gower sees his future wife as just part

---

[1] In using this expression, I am conflating the words of Edmund Burke (*Reflections on the Revolution in France*) concerning the "right" kinds of conservative English landscapes that can withstand the chaos of the French Revolution and Austen's own use of impertinence in describing the behavior of the gypsies on the road outside Highbury as they approached Harriet in *Emma*.

of the landscape which, he assumes, belongs to him.) Mary Crawford blends into the landscape as well. "A young woman, pretty, lively, with a harp as elegant as herself; and both placed near a window, cut down to the ground, and opening on a little lawn, surrounded by shrubs in the rich foliage of summer, was enough to catch any man's heart" (65). However, unlike the other unsuspecting female objects in the landscape, we can see Mary contriving this scene as she imagines Edmund seeing her framed attractively by the window and surrounding foliage.

Rose further claims that "rarely do the women in landscape images look out from the canvas at the viewer as an equal" (96). However, in these two novels, the heroines observe and reflect upon the significance of the landscape, yet feel comfortable within it. They obviously appreciate the sense of place in which they exist as well as use it to their advantage; Austen never turns them into figures strictly to be gazed upon in the landscape. The landscape is theirs; they maintain the best of the insider and outsider position.[2]

In order to gain a further understanding of how landscape functions historically from both an insider's and outsider's view, we can look again to the geographers. Assuming control over their world becomes a major theme for philosophers, poets, and painters during the eighteenth century. Cosgrove, in *Landscape and Social Formation*, notes a movement toward control over the landscape that favors an outsider's view. Landscape, according to Cosgrove, moves from concentration on someone within the landscape, an insider where "there is no clear separation of self from scene, subject from object" (19) to the spectator owning the view. As Cosgrove explains this position:

> The experience of the insider, the landscape as subject, and the collective life within it are all implicitly denied. Subjectivity is rendered the property of the artist and the viewer—those who control the landscape—not those who belong to it. (26)

This element of control of landscape is heightened by linear perspective, which gives the impression of freezing a moment in history. Figures seem scarcely noticeable in the landscape paintings—"in but not of their surroundings" (26). "Perspective locates the subject outside the landscape and stresses the unchanging objectivity of what is observed therein" (27), according to Cosgrove. However, a problem exists in that "landscape is object and subject both personally and socially" (20). Regardless of how much the aestheticians, poets, and improvers try to wrest control of the landscape as object for their personal use, an undercurrent of the insider relating analogically to the landscape remains in the arts. Particularly in the novels by women beginning in the late eighteenth century, and continuing into the nineteenth century as well, the woman within the landscape persists. Certainly the sense of the narrators and heroines of *Mansfield Park* and *Emma* retain that

---

[2] Rosemarie Bodenheimer, in "Looking at the Landscape in Jane Austen" (*Studies in English Literature*: 1981), contends that the language of landscape reflects character in Austen's novels and that "in this context the descriptions of landscape acquire metaphorical resonance largely through a relatively simple scheme in which spatial terms function also as perceptual and emotional ones" (610). I am more interested in the position of the heroine in her landscape than in characterization suggested by the language of landscape; however, Bodenheimer's suggestion that the female characters take what works for them emotionally from the landscape remains an important concept to consider.

undercurrent of subjective, insider relationship to the landscape. Fanny "belongs" to Mansfield; Emma "belongs" to Highbury.

And who "controls" the landscape during the eighteenth century? A sense of "taste" for landscape develops during this period. This "taste," according to art historian and critic John Barrell consists of "more refined judgment than can be acquired by those who practice a particular trade, and whose narrow interests afford them no general view of the world" (130)—in other words, the controllers are gentlemen. In fact, Barrell states that the power to generalize ideas and draw conclusions (as poets were attempting with their landscapes) was generally thought to be an intellectual act beyond most women.[3] Even women intellectuals of the time, like Hannah More, felt that women were limited, at least by their education. In her *Strictures on the Modern System of Female Education*, More's image of feminine academic performances is something like salads—"spontaneous productions of a fruitful but shallow soil" (13).

The eighteenth-century experience of landscape exhibits a history of masculine control of what many times turns out to be a very feminine landscape. Gone is the *locus amoenus*—lovely place—of Chaucer which Karl Kroeber calls "enchanting because it is naturalistically unlocatable and, because unlocalized, free from temporal complexities" (83). Instead of an insider relationship with the landscape characterized by Cosgrove's feudal economy where time and material production are unimportant, the eighteenth-century prospect viewer wants to locate the landscape geographically and frame it, observe it rather than interact with it and place it within a political history. In Fanny and Emma, we find heroines who interact with their landscapes and experience them emotionally, as well as locate themselves in a moral and socio-cultural landscape. They recognize what is "out-of-place" and move toward what Cosgrove defines as real landscape—a unity of people and environment.

***

Does Fanny "Make" the Place—Or—Does the Place "Make" Fanny?

Early in *Mansfield Park*, the Bertrams discuss sending Fanny to live with her Aunt Norris in White house. Lady Bertram carelessly tosses off the following comment concerning Fanny's expected move: "It can make very little difference to you, whether you are in one house or in the other" (25). But it *does* make a difference. Fanny has been at Mansfield Park only a short while, and yet she feels extremely connected to this place, exclaiming to her cousin, Edmund, "If I could suppose my aunt really to care for me, it would be delightful to feel myself of consequence to any body!—*Here*, I know am of none, and yet I love the place so well" (27). Edmund attempts to reassure her that she will have free access to the park and gardens, but Fanny needs to *live* at Mansfield Park and to be a part of it in a way she never could if she lived separately with Aunt Norris. Though she believes herself of little consequence to the family, Fanny loves the place and feels an

---

[3] John Barrell. *The Political Theory of Painting from Reynolds to Hazlitt*. New Haven: Yale UP, 1986.

almost spiritual connection to it. She says, "I love this house and everything in it" (26).

As Cresswell has stated, being "out of place" is both a powerful social and geographical metaphor. Fanny knows very clearly that her "place" is at Mansfield Park. Because Fanny knows her "place" at a deeply emotional and moral level, she is able both to transgress and transform that place, all the while retaining an awareness of the socio-cultural values of the estate at that time. When she refuses to marry Henry Crawford, standing firm even in the face of Sir Thomas's orders, she transgresses his rules and finds herself peremptorily exiled to Portsmouth. Portsmouth, even though she was born there, is clearly "out of place" for Fanny now. Upon her forced return to Portsmouth, she immediately knows the difference: "[S]he was at home. But alas! It was not such a home, she had not such a welcome as—she checked herself; she was unreasonable" (382). "Nobody was in their right place, nothing was done as it ought to be" (388-389). Gone was her enclave of civility.

Because of her deeply ingrained sense of Mansfield Park as *her* place (and perhaps an underlying sense of what *she* is to Mansfield Park), she can survive her exile and return to assist in the transformation of Mansfield Park. She, more than anyone else, recognizes the importance of Mansfield Park as a Burkean "enclave of civility," amidst the "clamorous impertinence" exhibited in other places such as London and Portsmouth.[4] On the trip back to Mansfield Park, all Fanny can talk about with her younger sister, Susan, are "the ways of Mansfield Park" and "a description of the people, the manners, [and] the amusements" (409). Finally, Fanny enters the park after three months' absence and is aware of the profound changes from winter until summer.

> Her eyes fell every where on lawns and plantations of the freshest green; and the trees, though not fully clothed, were in that delightful state, when farther beauty is known to be at hand, and when, while much is actually given to the sight, more yet remains for the imagination. (446-7)[5]

---

[4] In "'Enclaves of Civility amidst Clamorous Impertinence': Will as Reflected in the Landscape of *Emma*" (*European Romantic Review*: Winter 1997), I expand upon the connections between the landscape of *Emma* and the civic ideals of Edmund Burke, as espoused in *Reflections on the Revolution in France*. I write that "Jane Austen represents in *Emma*, the will and imagination of a character and their negative effects on the community" (95). Although Emma is the imaginist there, the same misuse of will and imagination occurs in *Mansfield Park*.

[5] What I see here as the potential transformative quality Fanny has/will have on Mansfield Park, Bodenheimer sees as a metaphor for Fanny's own metamorphosis into "one of those trees on the verge of full foliage" (618). However, I am somewhat uncomfortable with this interpretation because it reminds me of the woman as object in the landscape.

Douglas Murray, in "Spectatorship in *Mansfield Park*: Looking and Overlooking" (*Nineteenth-Century Literature* 1997) sees this scene as a way in which Fanny frames all her landscape views, as with a Claude glass, basically leaving out what is disturbing at Mansfield Park, "wrest[ing] a happy ending out of such unpromising material" (12). This interpretation does not hold if one believes, as I do, that Fanny is situated in a liminal position, one which gives her the confidence to believe she can help transform the landscape into all that it is capable of being.

While Emma's imaginative thinking about landscape needs moral correction, Austen suggests to the reader that Fanny's well-regulated moral imagination will continue to transform Mansfield Park.[6]

Although we never see Fanny with less than a strong sense of what is wrong and what is right, she does become increasingly aware of what "place" really means to her. Early in the novel, her cousins ridicule her for not being able to "put the map of Europe together" (18). She is just beginning her education. Jane Austen, from her earliest writing, places considerable emphasis on education in geography. In *Emma*, Harriet thinks that Frank Churchill might pass through Bath on his way from Yorkshire to Oxford to Highbury in Surrey; however, even the thought of such a great detour reveals Harriet's ignorance of geography—which for her mentor Emma "did not augur much" (189). Fanny does, however, quickly grasp a knowledge of the geography around her; she may not know yet which way to Ireland, but, being from Portsmouth, she knows where the Isle of Wight is, calling it "the Island," much to her cousin's consternation.

As Fanny grows older, her attachment to Mansfield Park only deepens. It seems to be a source of her physical and spiritual strength, even though she is not beloved by all its inhabitants. Mrs. Grant describes Mansfield Park as a "cure." She assures Mary and Henry Crawford, "Mansfield shall cure you both—and without any taking in. Stay with us and we will cure you" (47). Mrs. Grant may be referring to a cure for cynicism—a moral cure for Mary's jaundiced attitude toward matrimony. Mansfield itself as a place does constitute a "cure," but one that will work only if a person lets it. This influence might be described as the kind Edmund Burke has in mind as he describes the best kind of civil and religious system. He writes that the "sense of mankind" is like a

> provident proprietor [who] preserves the structure from profanation and ruin, as a sacred temple, purged from all impurities of fraud and violence and injustice and tyranny, hath solemnly and forever consecrated the commonwealth, and all that officiate in it. (467)

His sense of an enclave of civility as a place preserved and conserved by the owners and inhabitants seems in keeping with how Jane Austen envisions Mansfield Park. The people who come here must want the "cure." Fanny's sister, Susan, "who had an innate taste for the genteel and well-appointed" (419), is already predisposed to the "cure" of Mansfield Park. However, Henry and Mary, "without wanting to be cured, were very willing to stay" (47). In fact, the reader learns that, before even meeting the Crawfords, "To any thing like a permanence of abode, or limitation of society, Henry Crawford had, unluckily, a great dislike" (41), and Mary easily wearied of staying in one place. To be cured, one must yearn for permanence. The only character here who welcomes the cure from the start and is entirely ready to be purged from all impurities is Fanny.

---

[6] In "Placement and Replacement in *Mansfield Park*" (*U of Toronto Quarterly*, vol. 54, no. 3, pp. 221-233), F. T. Flahiff argues the importance of place for itself, not just a backdrop or symbol for characters. He asserts that Mansfield Park will survive even without Fanny. I believe it will; however, Fanny still has a transformative quality, recognizable by many of the inhabitants, that significantly improves the estate.

Contrasting Mary's sense of landscape with that of Fanny helps the reader understand how Jane Austen intends her true heroines to react to their proper surroundings. In one scene, Mary "courts" Fanny in the shrubbery of the Grant parsonage, and Fanny explains how she feels about the landscape in a way that places the landscape within her in the form of memory and suggests a palimpsest of past and future landscapes:

> Every time I come into this shrubbery I am more struck with its growth and beauty. Three years ago, this was nothing but a rough hedgerow along the upper side of the field, never thought of as any thing, or capable of becoming any thing; and now it is converted into a walk, and it would be difficult to say whether most valuable as a convenience or an ornament; and perhaps in another three years we may be forgetting—almost forgetting what it was before. How wonderful, how very wonderful the operations of time, and the changes of the human mind! (208)

Unlike Fanny, who can both observe the landscape and internalize it—be both in and out, Mary is not quite as rhapsodic. She says, "To say the truth, ... I am something like the famous Doge at the court of Lewis XIV; and may declare that I see no wonder in this shrubbery equal to seeing myself in it" (209-10). Now, of course, Mary is commenting on finding herself in such a rural setting, lacking the excitement and stimulation of London, but she is also placing herself as an object in the landscape, much as though she were observing herself as the male landscape proprietor might observe her. Fanny takes the landscape in as a cure; whereas Mary simply sees herself objectified in the shrubbery. Fanny internalizes the landscape, as is shown as she travels to Sotherton: "Her own thoughts and reflections were habitually her best companions; and in observing the appearance of the country ... the state of the harvest, the cottages, the cattle, she found entertainment" (80). Mary, on the other hand, "saw nature, inanimate nature, with little observation: her attention was all for men and women" (81). However the cure here involves noticing and internalizing the landscape, not simply skimming over it superficially.

Or—Is Fanny the "cure" for Mansfield Park, once Sir Thomas leaves and the other characters start using their imaginations wrongly to "profane the temple"? Mansfield Park, is "a park, a real park five miles round, a spacious modern-built house, so well placed and well screened as to deserve to be in any collection of engravings of gentlemen's seats in the kingdom"—this according to Mary Crawford's first impressions (48). And so we receive a quintessential eighteenth-century proprietor's outsider view of the place, even going so far as to imagine it as a framed engraving, quite the Claude glass framed image. Interestingly, shortly after this description of the park is given from Mary's mind, Mary meets Fanny and immediately asks, "Pray, is she out, or is she not?" (48). Of course, this question concerns Fanny's formal coming-of-age introduction to society, but if we examine such a question, as Cresswell would—from the geographical aesthetical point of view, we might see Fanny as in a liminal place—neither "in" nor "out" of place.

The concept of liminality has been discussed in connection with Austen's juvenile piece, "Catharine—Or the Bower." However, liminality might be associated with the "cure" as well as "'betwixt and between' moments when people are disposed to feel liberated from the norms of society" (Hughes 23). Shields writes:

the liminal status of the eighteenth-century seashore as an ill-defined margin between land and sea fitted well with the medical notion of the "cure" ... As a physical threshold, a limen, the beach has been difficult to dominate, providing the basis for its "outsider" position. (qtd. in Hughes 23)

Fanny's position as simultaneously insider and outsider, as curative and inflexible, fits well with the geographical description of limen as outsider. Also, her liminal position makes her difficult to dominate, even by Sir Thomas. Her cousin and closest friend, Edmund, cannot quite pin her position. He tells Mary, "She has the age and sense of a woman, but the outs and not outs are beyond me" (49). Fanny's liminal position in the landscape of Mansfield Park indicates she is in a position to effect its cure. In fact, Fanny cures by her very existence.

Fanny's station in the wilderness at Sotherton represents an example of prospect/refuge in the landscape and one where Fanny is situated liminally. As all the young people explore the grounds at Sotherton, they find that the "lawn [is] bounded on each side by a high wall" and the terrace walk is "backed by iron palisades" (85). The restrictions of the landscape here only present a challenge for most of them. In the course of their exploration of the grounds, Mary, Edmund, and Fanny find an unlocked door, leading to a "nice little wood" (91). In this edge-of-the-wood refuge, Fanny finds out more about what is going on around her than any of the other characters, who are dashing about losing themselves and any prospect they might have had on the scene. As Fanny herself puts it: "To sit in the shade on a fine day, and look upon verdure, is the most perfect refreshment" (96). She can appreciate the landscape more from her stationary position than the others do as they move about restlessly.

As the moral center of the novel, Fanny sits on a bench in this zone of safety and comes in contact with the others and is the only one of all who actually retains both prospect and refuge by remaining in a liminal position between the two. Mary and Edmund leave to "determine the dimensions of the woods by walking a little more about it" (96). Twenty minutes later Henry, Maria, and Mr. Rushworth arrive, pause to express sympathy for Fanny, whom they perceive as lonely, and then find an iron gate, this time a locked one. This situation gives Maria a chance to rid herself of Rushworth, as he must go back for the key. When Rushworth is gone, Henry and Maria discuss her "prospects"—"a very smiling scene" (99). Maria asks:

> Do you mean literally or figuratively? Literally, I conclude. Yes, certainly, the sun shines and the park looks very cheerful. But unluckily that iron gate, that ha-ha, give me a feeling of restraint and hardship. I cannot get out, as the starling said. (99)

Crawford replies:

> I think you might with little difficulty pass round the edge of the gate, here with my assistance; I think it might be done, if you really wished to be more at large, and could allow yourself to think it not prohibited. (99)

The whole scene here is about in's and out's, socially (and morally) correct behavior as illustrated by everyone's movement in the landscape. Prospects are clearly described as having double meanings—the future of the character and the geographical view. The literal scene becomes a way of predicting plot. Maria sees herself as the starling of Laurence Sterne's *Sentimental Journey*, and Henry is the one who helps her out of her cage, the walled-in part of Sotherton. He encourages her to use her own will to decide what is "prohibited" and what is not. This landscape, in fact, predicts the future moral dilemma that will face Maria as she must decide whether to stay with her husband or use Henry's "assistance" to leave Rushworth.

Fanny, meanwhile, continues to occupy her position on the bench at the edge of the walled-in area of the wilderness. Her place allows her to know everything that is happening and gives her the opportunity of clearly pronouncing on the true morality of the situation: "You will certainly hurt yourself against those spikes—you will tear your gown—you will be in danger of slipping into the ha-ha. You had better not go," Fanny warns Maria, who ignores her (99-100). Julia comes by Fanny, seated on her bench, clearly irritated at being left behind. Mr. Rushworth returns and, disheartened, turns to Fanny for sympathy. So Fanny remains in a position of having a "prospect" on the general affairs of the others, and yet, a sense of refuge on a bench at the edge of the wood. She may not be happy, but at least she is safe in her sense of propriety. Neither of the chaperones, Mrs. Rushworth or Mrs. Norris, knows the unaccompanied couples, Mary and Edmund and Maria and Henry, have spent at least an hour alone in a distant part of the estate. Fanny, however, in her liminal position, has been privy to the comings and goings of them all. She afterwards observed that "since the day at Sotherton, she could never see Mr. Crawford with either sister without observation, and seldom without wonder or censure" (142). This scene, of course, does not take place in Mansfield Park (although Fanny does approve of Sotherton and does not want it modernized). However, the setting does illustrate how Fanny situates herself in a position to achieve both a good sense of prospect and also some degree of refuge in a seat by the edge of the woods. In a way, she carries her own little enclave of civility with her here.

Although the amateur theatrical production of "Lovers' Vows" does not directly concern landscape, it does give the reader a good indication of Fanny's position, again neither in nor out—this time, of the play. Prior to the instigation of the theatricals, Fanny shows her unambiguous connections to the landscape, explaining how certain landscapes make her believe that there might be "neither wickedness nor sorrow in the world" (113). She makes a clear connection between emotionally evocative landscape and morality. But Edmund, who has agreed with her and kept her company as they look at the harmony and repose of "an unclouded night, and the contrast of the deep shade of the woods" as seen through the window (113) is lured by the siren sound of Mary's harp-playing. It is only a matter of time before Tom's friend, John Yates, arrives, and Fanny must stand at the threshold again, so to speak, and watch an "unnatural" and artificial drama take place, one which gives everyone permission to act in ways that ignore what is morally acceptable and one which threatens Mansfield Park itself as an enclave of civility.

The problem here is not theatricals per se—the Austen family and relatives had enthusiastically participated in these themselves—but the way in which this particular play allows Mary to make love to Edmund and Maria to Henry. Just as picturesque landscape improvements were not condemned out of hand by Austen, so such improvements might be criticized if venerable avenues of oaks were eliminated or the church were separated from the estate. Both suggest misplaced motives. As Mr. Rushworth was willing to "improve" Sotherton, even if the improvements might threaten the venerable conservative nature of the place, so Tom Bertram is only too willing to alter Mansfield Park. He turns the billiard room into a theater and Sir Thomas's room into a green room, though such improvements threaten the innate moral standards of that place, with Edmund knowing that their "father would totally disapprove it" (126). Alistair Duckworth best characterizes the true dangers of the theater at Mansfield Park as it symbolizes "moral confusion of the actors and the confusion that their acting has introduced into an ordered social structure" (56-57).

As in the Sotherton landscape, Fanny remains "a quiet auditor of the whole" (136), and, as at Sotherton, she is placed in a position to watch the action. This position is the cottage-by-the-wood one—speaking in terms of landscape aesthetics—a good place to hide and a good place to seek. Ironically, the other actors press Fanny to take the part of cottager's wife, and, of course, she refuses. The "cottage" to which Fanny does have recourse as a place where "she could go ... after any thing unpleasant below, and find immediate consolation" (151) is the old school room, now called the East-room, her "nest of comforts" (152), to use a term very close to one used by philosopher Gaston Bachelard. (In many ways this room has the same effect as Kitty's bower has on Kitty. And, like Kitty, Fanny uses her refuge as a place to read, transporting herself away from the present problematic landscape to the more exotic one of China.)[7] Close to her little white attic that had been early assigned as Fanny's bedroom, the East-room even has prospects in the form of transparencies on the windows, picturesque scenes of Tintern Abbey, a cave in Italy, and a moonlight lake in Cumberland, all very like those Gilpin would approve as suitable for viewing with a Claude glass. Both the white attic and the East-room act as the "safe places" for Fanny, her "cottage" within Mansfield Park. The zone of safety, symbolized by a cottage, becomes a dream shared with her brother William. They imagine sharing a cottage after William leaves the navy and has the prize money to buy a small place.

Bachelard discusses how small spaces, such as Fanny's little unheated rooms, and large spaces, such as a park "five miles round" interact. "The two kinds of space, intimate space and exterior space, keep encouraging each other, as it were, in their growth" (201). Fanny's reflections in her "intimate space" have a strong effect on her strength of feeling and behavior in the exterior space, both the "sublimity of nature" as seen through the window of the drawing room at Mansfield Park and the "improvements" of the larger part of the house for the play. The theater (billiard room) becomes a place of exposure—in more ways than one. But in the school room, Fanny "was beyond their reach" (157). Fanny might have stayed in her "cottage," but she chose to step out of it into a position just at the edge of the action, not taking part in the play but as a "very courteous listener" (164) and invisible observer of the action. She could have retreated to her refuge, her "nest of

---

[7] In *The Poetics of Space* (NY: Orion P, 1964), Gaston Bachelard entitles a chapter "Nests." He asserts that nests take us back to childhood and that they provide "primal images" where "the human being likes to 'withdraw into his corner,' and that it gives him physical pleasure to do so" (91).

comforts," but instead she stubbornly stays on the sideline of the play, reading it, memorizing much of it, torturing herself by knowing the romantic parts Mary and Edmund will play with each other. She even asks herself "why had not she rather gone to her own room, she had felt to be safest, instead of attending the rehearsal at all?" (172) She comes so close to entering the world of the play itself that she has just agreed to read the cottager's wife's part in rehearsal as Sir Thomas returns home to discover the inappropriate behavior of his family. But she has resisted all of this time, and Edmund defends Fanny's behavior to his father:

> Fanny is the only one who has judged rightly throughout, who has been consistent. *Her* feelings have been steadily against it from first to last. She never ceased to think of what was due to you. You will find Fanny everything you could wish. (187)

But Sir Thomas *wishes* Fanny would accept Henry Crawford. When Fanny refuses, she is "exposed" to Portsmouth. Morally dangerous landscapes for Austen are usually found in cities. London, of course, is the worst. Mr. Woodhouse is not the only character to find London suspect. Edmund earlier has objected to Mary Crawford when she tells him that London speaks for the nation. He replies, "We do not look in great cities for our best morality. It is not there that respectable people of any denomination can do most good" (93). Tom almost dies in London after a bout of drinking followed by a fall. The real transgressions committed by Maria and Julia Bertram occur in the licentious freedom of London, and there the Crawfords' true personalities are revealed.

Fanny, however, almost succumbs to the charms of Henry Crawford in Portsmouth, for her, a zone of exposure. She is just on the edge, after he has come to Portsmouth to convince her that he has changed and has become more morally responsible than she had thought before. Tellingly, she mentions this information in terms of Mansfield Park. "It was parting with somebody of the nature of a friend; and though in one light glad to have him gone, it seemed as if she was now deserted by everybody; it was a sort of renewed separation from Mansfield" (413).

The only way in which Fanny could be so strongly tempted by Henry is to be positioned in a landscape with no refuge and all exposure. She was home, but her birthplace was not a home to her, and she is constantly reminded of that fact. The disorder of the Price household affected her the most. This house was "in almost every respect, the very reverse of what she could have wished. It was the abode of noise, disorder, and impropriety. Nobody was in their right place as it ought to be" (388-9). It is, in fact, all "clamorous impertinence." So she could only think back on Mansfield, "the elegance, propriety, regularity, harmony—and perhaps above all, the peace and tranquility" (391).[8] Now, except for the elegance, Mansfield Park did not always have these other positive attributes; however, the ideal of order was one that Sir Thomas strove for at Mansfield Park. No one in the Price household had any idea of what "order" was. For Fanny, "though Mansfield Park might have some pains, Portsmouth could have no pleasures" (392). She had no "nest of comforts" in the room she shared with her sister; it only reminded her of the East-room by its lack of a fire.

---

[8] Humphry Repton strives for these same characteristics for his landscape. Obviously Austen did admire many of the same traits as Repton in her landscapes.

The real landscape of exposure at Portsmouth lay beyond the Price house. When Henry comes to visit Fanny, the walk along the ramparts puts Fanny in the greatest danger because, with little opportunity to reflect, she must see Henry Crawford, literally, in the best possible light.

> The day was uncommonly lovely ... every thing looked so beautiful under the influence of such a sky ... with the ever-varying hues of the sea now at high water, dancing in its glee and dashing against the ramparts with so fine a sound, produced altogether such a combination of charms for Fanny, as made her gradually almost careless of the circumstances. (409)

In some ways there is a similarity between this landscape of exposure and the one on the Cobb at Lyme Regis in *Persuasion*. With the sea comes exposure (as well as the position of liminality in the landscape). Fortunately, Fanny is wiser than Louisa Musgrove and does not impulsively respond to Henry Crawford. His sister Mary's humorous description of the "delightful walk" makes the reader aware of the different ways in which the landscape may be interpreted. First Mary relates what Henry has told her about the "balmy air, the sparkling sea" (415), but later in the same letter she warns Fanny about "those vile sea-breezes" being "the ruin of beauty" (416), reminding the reader of Sir Walter Elliot's criticism of sailors' complexions.

Fortunately for Fanny, she does not have to remain in Portsmouth, all "clamorous impertinence" and certainly a landscape that exposes Fanny to the susceptibility to Henry's charms in a way she had not experienced at Mansfield Park. But Mansfield Park needs Fanny's presence to affect a cure for the sick and distraught Bertrams. The licentious atmosphere of London has encouraged them to do what they had only wanted to do in the past. Maria has run away with Henry, causing scandal to herself and her family. Julia has eloped with a less than ideal husband. Now that the Crawfords are away from Mansfield Park, they feel freer to act with even more "impertinence." Mary has shown her lack of sensitivity and moral scruples. Edmund was the most upset by her concern not for the shame that her brother and Maria have brought on themselves and the pain caused to others, but as Edmund tells Fanny, "she saw it as folly, and that folly stamped only by exposure" (455). "Her's are faults of principle ... a corrupted, vitiated mind" (456). Now everyone left at Mansfield Park needs Fanny. Fanny may not be the cure, but her presence has definite curative value for those who want it. She leaves "the barriers of Portsmouth" (445) and returns to "the Park, her perceptions and her pleasures ... of the keenest sort" (446). Mansfield Park might have gone on without Fanny Price. Her ability to internalize the landscape of such a place strengthens both the place and the people who live there. She fully recognizes Mansfield Park as an "enclave of civility."

***

"The Most Natural Thing in the World": What is "Natural" in Emma?

> "Nothing in life requires more attention than the things that appear to be natural." (Balzac *La rabouilleuse*)

What is "only natural" in *Emma*? The expression "only natural" is mentioned so frequently and so casually in this novel that we might wonder about it. The word "natural," used more than fifty times in the novel, shifts in meaning from Harriet Smith being the "natural child of somebody," therefore "illegitimate," (22) to the lessening intimacy between Harriet and Emma after they are both married. It subsides in "the most gradual, natural manner" in the ordinary course of events (482). As she tries to bring Harriet and Mr. Elton together romantically, Emma stops on the footpath to adjust her bootlace. A child comes along and it seems to her "the most natural thing in the world, or would have been the most natural, had she been acting just then without design" (88) to go along with the child. In this scene we begin to realize that when "natural" means "by design," something is wrong. Emma frequently describes Harriet as having "all those natural graces," and the match with Elton Emma sees as "only too palpably desirable, natural, and probable, for her to have much merit in planning it" (34-35).

Much of the action in *Emma* is forwarded by the "unnatural" that one of the characters insists is "natural." Looking at Tim Cresswell's ideas about what is natural in geography, we, as readers, might find a helpful way of examining what is "natural" in *Emma*. Because place, as Cresswell asserts, "is not simply a geographical matter ... [and] always intersects with sociocultural expectations" (8), we will be looking at the word "natural" used with characters and with place in combination. Cresswell writes: "An ideology that seeks to conceal its own historical roots uses the physical naturalness of place to make claims about the essential nature of place" (160). What or who is really "natural" and what or who is concealing the truth? These are important questions to ask about the landscape of *Emma*.

Besides Emma's use of natural to move along her match-making plots for Harriet, other characters are associated with the word as well. Let us consider Frank Churchill. The word "natural" is used in reference to him many times in the novel. The first mention of his arrival in Highbury causes an argument between Emma and Mr. Knightley. Emma says, "What has Mr. Frank Churchill done, to make you suppose him such an unnatural creature?" Mr. Knightley replies,

> I am not supposing him at all an unnatural creature, in suspecting that he may have learnt to be above his connections, and to care very little for any thing but his own pleasure from living with those who have always set him the example of it. It is a great deal more natural than one could wish. (145)

Mr. Knightley points out the real meaning of "natural," reminding Emma of the true background of Frank Churchill.

Everything surrounding the Churchill/Fairfax plot is "natural"—and therefore, a cover-up. The piano was a gift from Colonel Campbell, "the most natural thing in the world." Frank makes what he calls a "natural" visit to the Bates home—at least, this is what Emma tells herself when she is surprised to find him there (261). It was "natural" for Emma to visit Jane; it was "natural" for Frank "that he had cause to sigh." His letter to Emma was "natural and honorable." These uses of "natural" are ironic ones, referring, as the reader eventually learns, to the duplicity of Frank Churchill and the rampant imagination he encourages in Emma. When Emma *chooses* to find that events are natural, then, for her at least, they are.

Mrs. Elton is another character associated with the word "natural." "Her Bath habits made evening parties perfectly natural to her." She claims for herself "natural taste," which we the readers "naturally" doubt. And, of course, the famous strawberry party suggested by Mrs. Elton is supposed to be "natural." She tells "Knightley," as she calls him with unnatural familiarity, "We are to walk about your gardens, and gather the strawberries ourselves, and sit under trees,—or whatever else you may like to provide, it is to be all out of doors—a table spread in the shade, you know. Every thing as natural and simple as possible" (355). Mr. Knightley, the "real" authority on how "natural" shall be regarded, recognizes Mrs. Elton's idea of natural *al fresco* dining as "unnatural" for human beings, who, he believes, should dine in a more civilized manner indoors. "My idea of the simple and the natural will be to have the table spread in the dining-room. The nature and the simplicity of gentlemen and ladies, with their servants and furniture, I think is best observed by meals within doors" (355). Again, Mr. Knightley's more practical notion of what is natural is the one we are meant to admire; Mrs. Elton's idea of natural is contrived, and as an outsider to the landscape of Highbury and its surroundings, she has not earned the right to decide what can be natural there. (She probably envisions herself in a highly flattering pose in a landscape by Fragonard.) Alistair Duckworth comments on Mr. Knightley's definition of "natural": "To be natural, that is, is to behave socially, to act in accordance with accustomed usages. Nature and culture are not, for Knightley, opposed but complementary terms" ("Nature" 317).

In a way, Emma, Frank Churchill, and Mrs. Elton can be seen as landscape improvers. Emma tries to improve and call "natural" the landscapes that Harriet might call home. Frank is found in places he should not be found, and yet he implies that his presence is "natural" there. Mrs. Elton contrives various scenes for the residents at Highbury, such as the Strawberry Party and the trip to Box Hill. Improvement is not always flawed; however, the right kinds of improvements enhance the landscape and improve upon its naturalness. Let us consider Humphry Repton. Austen takes a jab at him in *Mansfield Park*, but, as a novelist, she tries some of the same methods herself to "improve" the landscape for the heroine, similar to the way that Repton improved the landscape on behalf of dozens of gentlemen landowners.[9] John Dixon Hunt links Austen and Repton in the following observation: "Repton's demand of a landscape that it satisfy the mind's understanding of its schemes as well as the eyes' pleasure links him firmly, as it does Jane Austen, with certain eighteenth-century predecessors" (166). One of these predecessors was Edmund Burke, who believed in a combination of preservation and adaptation in English institutions. Ann Bermingham argues that attitudes of Burke about government and human nature affect landscape design and that the "point of the picturesque aesthetic was not simply to build new gardens ... but rather to preserve old gardens that were already picturesque" (82); in other words, Repton strives for what preserves the past and ties it to the present—a new natural landscape.

---

[9] John Dixon Hunt [*Gardens and the Picturesque* (Cambridge: MIT P, 1992)] "finds Austen's rejection of Repton ... puzzling" (357), since, for the most part, Austen's and Repton's aesthetics closely parallel each other. Hunt suggests that Repton was more conservative than Duckworth would have readers believe.

Improvements for Austen in *Emma* can be natural in the sense of "improved" in the most discerning, conservative Reptonian way of a Mr. Knightley.[10] Or, improvements can be "natural" in the sense of "contrived," as in Mrs. Elton's notion of the strawberry party. She sees herself with her large bonnet and beribboned strawberry basket as the central focus of the landscape. Based upon the "before" and "after" pictures in his professional Red Books (works of art in themselves, as well as persuasive marketing devices), Repton attempts to take a scene as it is now, call it "unnatural," and then artificially "naturalize it." Austen creates "enclaves of civility" that express what she considers the appropriate traits: preservation and adaptation. Humphry Repton was a painter and a poet, as well as a landscape architect. As a result, he was concerned that his gardens, as his other artistic works, express many characteristics connected with these traits: Congruity, Utility, Order, Symmetry, Picturesque Effect, Intricacy, Simplicity, Variety, Contrast, Continuity, Association, Grandeur, Appropriation, Animation, and the Seasons (Laurie, *Humphry Repton* 42). For Repton, these characteristics expressed the "natural." Many of Austen's novelistic landscape descriptions take into account most, if not all, of these characteristics. Emma changes a scene and calls it "natural." Repton similarly finds that eliminating unpleasant aspects of the landscape and adding pleasant ones provides a new "naturalness" not originally in the scene. Early in his career, he asserted that his image of the English garden balanced "the happy medium between the wilderness of nature and the stiffness of art" (qtd. from Daniels, *Humphry Repton* 114). In a similar manner, Austen improves upon the natural; however, she also uses "natural" as a warning to the reader. Some "natural" responses are anything but natural. Thus we can assess some scenes in *Emma* as "enclaves of civility," while others illustrate "clamorous impertinence."

Jane Austen was visiting Mrs. Austen's cousin, Reverend Thomas Leigh, when he learned that he had inherited Stoneleigh Abbey. No doubt, during the Austens' visit in 1806, they discussed Repton's advice upon planning a new drive at Aldestrop, where he presently lived, and the future improvements for Stoneleigh Abbey. Repton commented on the site, "I look upon Stoneleigh Abbey as a place *sui generis* and not to be compared to any other place" (qtd. in Batey 31). Although the

---

[10] Jill Heydt-Stevenson ("Liberty, Connection, and Tyranny: The Novels of Jane Austen and the Aesthetic Movement of the Picturesque," *Lessons of Romanticism: A Critical Companion*. Eds. Thomas Pfau and Robert F. Gleckner, Durham: Duke UP, 1998) deals with the convergence of construction of womanhood, national identity, and landscape. She believes that Austen aligned herself more with the landscape aestheticians (Price and Knight) rather than with the improver, Repton. Although I agree that Austen's heroines find freedom in certain kinds of landscape, I think Austen finds a way of allowing her heroines greater freedom within the improved estates, based upon their increasing awareness of their power there. Hedyt-Stevenson compares the freeing, natural aspects of picturesque landscape with the "unfettered" woman. My view of the landscape allows for women to find solace there, but they also have the ability to see themselves as separate from the landscape. I agree with Hedyt-Stevenson when she argues that Austen takes the "picturesque" and uses such landscapes to the advantage of her heroines. The picturesque aesthetic "highlights not 'framing' but the play between the frame and chaos: in the aesthetic and in the novels, the paradox of the copy and the original is unresolvable, for we cannot determine whether the landscape or the landscape sketch came first, since art and nature are engaged in a process of reflexive influence" (270). I believe that both Repton and Austen work with this notion of the interplay between natural and artistic landscape.

improvements Repton suggested and implemented for Stoneleigh Abbey changed the original lay of the land, they are considered some of the most important of Repton's work. Landscape historian, Mavis Batey describes such an enclave of civility:

> Much of the landscape he designed [at Stoneleigh Abbey] is still to be seen today. The Avon was widened and brought nearer the house, the cattle across the river being separated by a natural barrier rather than a deceptive ha-ha; a shrubbery wilderness walk led down from the terrace to his weir; ... from a perimeter walk around the brow of a hill framed views were made of the house, weir and island in the tradition of Gilpin's picturesque "stations." (31)

Repton ultimately implements improvements at Stoneleigh Abbey that look as though they were always there and which naturally *belong* to the landscape.

Both Repton's and Austen's landscape descriptions resemble pictures; in fact, Repton's scenes of Stoneleigh resemble a combination of scenes by Watteau and Claude. This plan and others are meant to lead the visitor from one view to the next; however, Repton's plans move toward the views which seem less artificial and more natural than those of his predecessors, William Kent and Capability Brown. Most of his Red Books, besides the sketches, illustrating "before" and "after" scenes, have written descriptions of approaches, views, walks, and "distant objects for future consideration." In his *Plans, Sketches, and Hints for the Improvement of Ferne-Hall in the Countie of Salop*, Repton describes a series of views, one from the drawing room:

> The removal of the hedge C will alone almost let in the views of this Scene, but it may be effectually done by paring off a little of the ridge on which the hedge stands. I am sure that I am not deceiv'd in my expectations from this spot, because by bending aside a few boughs & breaking off twigs, I got a clear line of sight with the help of a telescope which I use for such purposes. This opening must be made to appear accidental, & not a hole cut thro' the wood on purpose.

The description of this view illustrates how important "only natural" was for Repton, as he uses a telescope to imagine what this scene will look like "framed," with a Gilpinesque opening, "appearing accidental."

Landscape is socially constructed in *Emma* and can be natural in the sense that it does not seem contrived. Sites such as Donwell Abbey, Highbury, Hartfield, and Randalls represent "enclaves of civility." They are natural because they represent England in its best sense, arising from the preservation of English history and culture. The "unnatural" sites all exist on the outside, the exposed landscape. They are all "clamorous impertinence." These landscapes are Box Hill, London, the road outside of Highbury where the gypsies linger, the fields where Jane wandered, or Maple Grove, home of the Sucklings. The unnatural, in some cases such as in Box Hill and the road through the woods, are actually not much touched by civilizing influence—or improvement.

Impertinence does not belong in the safe Burkean enclaves, those landscapes that reflect preservation and very gradual adaptation. Impertinence involves people unrestrained by the landscape. Both the gypsies and Mrs. Elton overstep the bounds of propriety, showing improper respect and ill manners; in fact, Austen uses "impertinent" to describe them both. People—and their intent—and the landscape cannot be extricated from one another. As Repton many times improves an estate by moving a few trees or changing the curve of a drive as he strives for the proper preservation and adaptation of the estate, Austen improves by illustrating how walking in the shrubbery at Hartfield or viewing the world according to Donwell Abbey provides the alert person, such as Emma, with a realization of what really is "the most natural thing in the world."

We need only look at Hartfield to understand the importance of place in *Emma*. Emma would not think of leaving it, even at the beginning of the novel when Mrs. Weston and Mr. Knightley agree Emma "is so happy at Hartfield" that they cannot imagine her entertaining matrimony if only because it would take her away from her home (41). Emma sets up an either/or situation where Harriet believes she will be forced to choose. Emma tells Harriet, "You are a great deal too necessary at Hartfield, to be spared to Abbey-Mill" (55). In fact, we know that the farm is an integral part of the estate at Donwell and, as such, is granted great importance by Mr. Knightley, that most important visitor to Hartfield. When brother John returns for a visit, he and George are happily absorbed

> and as a farmer, as keeping in hand the home-farm at Donwell, he [George] had to tell what every field was to bear next year, and to give all such local information as could not fail of being interesting to a brother whose home it had equally been the longest part of his life, and whose attachments were strong. (100)

We find that Harriet could do much worse than pick Abbey-Mill. Cosgrove writes, "Landscape [is] a way of seeing with its own history" (1), and Austen attributes this accretive history in the landscape to "true English style" (99).

The reader of Austen's *Emma* views enclaves of civility, contrasted with ones of clamorous impertinence, natural ones and unnatural ones, ones that provide safety for our heroine and ones that expose her and that teach her more deeply to appreciate the parts of the landscape which are truly her zones of safety. Here are some ways of perceiving the landscape, according to geographer J. B. Jackson that describe what underlies Jane Austen's landscape of *Emma*:

> Landscape is anchored in *human life*, not something to look at but to live in, and to live in socially. Landscape is a *unity* of people and environment which opposes in its reality the false dichotomy of man and nature ... Landscape is to be judged as a *place for living and working* in terms of those who actually do live and work there. All landscapes are *symbolic*, they express "a persistent desire to make the earth over in the image of some heaven," and they undergo *change* because they are expressions of society, itself making history through time.
>
> (qtd. in Cosgrove, *The Idea of Landscape*, 35)

Jackson's description represents a geographical ideal, one of a safe place in both the geographic sense and in the more philosophical sense of Edmund Burke.

However, not all landscapes offer this unity. The landscapes of exposure, unimproved, lacking in civility, all clamorous impertinence exist outside of Highbury and its satellite estates. Some of them, such as London, are clearly already "unnatural" or contrived. Others, such as the roads and Box Hill are "natural" in that they are unimproved, but unnatural because of the actions of the people. London (which Mr. Woodhouse, for once rightly, sees as a generally threatening place to the health of his daughter and grandchildren), Maple Grove, near the "very heart of Bristol," the exposed fields where Jane Fairfax wandered, the open road exposing young women to the threats of gypsies, and, finally, Box Hill, where Emma herself becomes the source of impertinence, all have potentially suspicious and dangerous characteristics. These places threaten Emma, as well as Jane and Harriet, whether they realize it or not.

London, in both *Mansfield Park* and *Emma*, is a site of exposure to sickness, both physical and moral. Mr. Woodhouse says, "The truth is, that in London it is always a sickly season. Nobody is healthy in London—no body can be" (103). London is always connected with Frank Churchill as well (when he is not connected with France, which is even worse). He is always traveling the sixteen miles there, even for something as trivial as a haircut. Maple Grove is suspect simply because Mrs. Elton's sister lives there, and Mrs. Elton cannot stop comparing it with Hartfield: "Very like Maple Grove indeed! She was quite struck by the likeness" (273). Since Hartfield was considered *sui generis*, to use Repton's term, Emma was horrified to have such an outsider place compared to it. Besides, Maple Grove was close to "the very heart of Bristol (183), home for Mrs. Elton, and long associated with the slave trade (also mentioned in *Emma*).

One of the clearest sites of exposure, unimproved, and easily subject to "clamorous impertinence" is the Richmond Road outside of Highbury, where Harriet and Miss Bickerton find themselves threatened by gypsies as they come to an area "deeply shaded by elms on each side ... [and] very retired" (333). Harriet, unable to make her escape, is "assailed by a half dozen children, headed by a stout woman and great boy, all clamourous and impertinent" (333). Frank Churchill, who frequents the roads, in his effort to conceal his secret engagement, rescues Harriet. The impertinence of the gypsies is shown as only slightly more dangerous than that of Mrs. Elton, but what is important in this landscape is its existence outside the social structure of the Highbury community; it is "out of place." Leaving Highbury, the shrubberies of Hartwell, or Donwell Abbey exposes the female characters, in this case, Harriet, to real risks.

Yet another major exposure scene is Box Hill. The narrator of *Emma* describes "a principle of separation" which is "too strong for any fine prospects" (367). At Box Hill, Emma does not recognize the hazardous zone of exposure—in this case, she is not subject to physical danger but to social censure for her cruel remarks made to Miss Bates in the presence of their friends. The landscape itself at Box Hill is surprisingly exposed. On the top of the hill there is little wood, and on one side, there is nothing but a vast exposed prospect with no refuge. On the other side of the hill is a tangle of woods and no prospect. The lack of the two in combination is what makes this scene a true zone of exposure for Emma. The landscape is exposed, the sense of community is jeopardized, and Emma's impertinent behavior to Miss Bates exposes her as one who lacks concern for someone less fortunate than she.

Box Hill illustrates J. B. Jackson's notion of the importance of landscape as a "unity of people and environment." But here, they are not "unified." The day is hot and the people are already predisposed to be irritable and irritated. There are no good prospects and instead of being "unified," there is a "principle of separation." Emma does not "belong" to this landscape, and the combination of people, such as Frank Churchill and the place, cause her to act in a way that hurts one of the mainstays of Highbury. As Fanny found herself in danger of capitulating to Henry Crawford in the exposed ramparts of Portsmouth, Emma finds herself emotionally exposed and censured at Box Hill. The important point of her behavior is that it can corrupt the community of Highbury. Mr. Knightley reminds her that others "would be entirely guided by *your* treatment of her [Miss Bates]" (375). Her exposure here could have effects on the community as a whole, the enclaves of civility.

Other enclaves of civility all center around Highbury. Hartfield, Randalls, and Donwell Abbey are satellites tethered to Highbury by a series of ancient paths. As Mrs. Elton comments, "The grounds of Hartfield were small, but pretty; and the house was modern and well-built" (272). Mr. Woodhouse feels Emma will be safe if she does not venture beyond the shrubbery of Hartfield. Real geographical connections exist between Highbury and the neighboring estates which influence much of the action in *Emma*. Not only does Hartfield "belong" to Highbury but Randalls adjoins the town, and Donwell Abbey is a mile away but connected by footpaths which Mr. Knightley is loath to change. Highbury becomes a kind of metonymy for all the people in it, and they have a kind of communal will and intelligence: "within half an hour [news of the gypsies] was known all over Highbury" (336).

If the best landscape is, as Jackson writes: "a *unity* of people and environment which opposes in its reality the false dichotomy of man and nature," then the best landscape in *Emma* is the view at Donwell Abbey. The ultimate Reptonian view of an enclave of civility, Donwell Abbey has the qualities Humphry Repton values in a landscape:

> It was hot; and after walking some time over the gardens in a scattered, dispersed way, scarcely any three together, they insensibly followed one another to the delicious shade of a broad avenue of limes, which stretching beyond the garden at an equal distance from the river, seemed the finish of the pleasure grounds.—It led to nothing; nothing but a view at the end of a low stone wall with high pillars, which seemed intended, in their erection, to give the appearance of an approach to the house, which never had been there. Disputable, however, as might be the taste of such a termination, it was in itself a charming walk, and the view which closed it extremely pretty.—The considerable slope at nearly the foot of which the Abbey stood, gradually acquired a steeper form beyond its grounds; and at half a mile distant was a bank of considerable abruptness and grandeur, well clothed with wood;—and at the bottom of this bank, favourably placed and sheltered, rose the Abbey-Mill farm, with meadow in front, and the river making a close handsome curve around it.
>
> It was a sweet view—sweet to the eye and the mind. English verdure, English culture, English comfort, seen under a sun bright, without being oppressive. (360)

In her description of Donwell Abbey, Austen brings together harmonious aspects of English community as expressed by landscape in a way which mirrors Burke's images of preservation and adaptation. Hunt (in *Gardens and the Picturesque*) refers to the description of Donwell Abbey as one which "embodies many of Repton's principles—the propriety of the buildings, the avoidance of overly calculated picturesque vistas, the retention of old timbers, and such formal features as avenues, together with the estate's exact appeal to the mind's judgment" (165).

Along with the description of Pemberley, the view from the pleasure grounds of Donwell Abbey is Austen's most influential landscape. Here, whether "disputable" or not, improvements have been made that Austen finds admirable. The view is the important thing here—"the low stone wall with high pillars" implies the expectation of a viewer for a house, but the prospect dominates here. In the prospect is community—the scattered viewers "naturally" come together. A sense of history and English culture saturates the scene, but more recent adaptations and a Gilpinesque framing of it enhance the scene. So the artistic and natural combine in a way to show Emma what the truly natural can be for her: a view that includes the gentry, the church, and the common yeomanry as integral to English society. As well, the scene suggests a true zone of safety for Emma, one where she will have refuge and prospect. With her trip to Box Hill occurring only the next day, Emma truly begins to understand what the natural landscape could mean for her and how it could teach her to recognize what is natural in the truest sense. Fanny recognizes Mansfield Park almost immediately as a special enclave of civility amidst "clamorous impertinence," but it takes time and exposure to the truly "unnatural" and "out of place" for Emma to understand the true value a landscape might have.

The increasing realization about where they belong, what home truly means to them, and how they can use this knowledge to strengthen their communities place Fanny and Emma in the best possible positions to find good prospects and refuges in their landscape. As we examine Jane Austen's last completed novel, *Persuasion*, we find a heroine older and more experienced. Anne Elliot reluctantly leaves her home, only to find that her connections with new landscapes lead her toward a very different way of life—life aboard a ship, leaving the domestic sphere altogether, gaining new freedom, while she shares her husband's naval pursuits. As Fanny and Emma close out the world and establish closer ties with home, the landscape of *Persuasion* opens onto a wider landscape—as well as seascape.

Chapter 6

The Geography of *Persuasion*

> A woman sees the world, as it were, from a little elevation in her own garden, whence she takes an exact survey of home scenes, but takes not in that wider range of distant prospects which he who stands on a loftier eminence commands.
> —Hannah More (*Strictures on the Modern System of Female Education* 25)

> Woman in the career of genius, is the Atalanta, who will risk losing the race by running out of her road to pick up the golden apple; while her male competitor, without, perhaps, possessing greater natural strength or swiftness, will more certainly attain his object, by being less exposed to the seductions of extraneous beauty, and will win the race by despising the bait. (*Strictures* 27)

> The big Bow-wow strain I can do myself like any now going, but the exquisite touch which renders ordinary commonplace things and characters interesting from the truth of the description and the sentiment is denied to me.
> —Walter Scott, concerning Austen's work in his March 14, 1826, journal entry

Besides Fanny Burney and Ann Radcliffe, another contemporary of Jane Austen who used landscape in her writing was Hannah More. Austen had ambiguous feelings for More. Austen biographer Park Honan believes that Austen "admired that skilful and vigorous woman who wanted to train the female intellect" (338). Honan also notes that Austen places More "at the centre of *Mansfield Park*" (338). Fanny Price does exemplify More's ideal for female education:

> Not that which smothers a woman with accomplishments, but that which tends to consolidate a firm and regular system of character ... not that which is made up of the shreds and patches of useless arts, but that which inculcates principles, polishes taste, [and] cultivates reason." (*Coelebs in Search of a Wife* 14)

Five years after writing to Cassandra about her own dislike of Evangelicals, Austen wrote to her niece, Fanny: "I am by no means convinced that we ought not all to be Evangelicals, and am at least persuaded that they who are so from Reason and Feeling, must be happiest and safest" (*Letters* 280). Here she seems to agree with More's principles; however, with Anne, Austen takes her own vision of what a woman can do much farther than does More.

Besides examining the landscape of *Persuasion* alongside that of More, we find some interesting contrasts with novelist Walter Scott. Both novelists admired each other. Austen writes to Cassandra concerning Scott's novels: "Walter Scott has no business to write novels, especially good ones.—It is not fair" (*Letters* 277). In an 1816 review of *Emma*, Scott wrote that her novel was "copy[ed] from nature as she really exists in the common walks of life, and presenting to the reader, instead of the splendid scenes of an imaginary world, a correct and striking representation of that which is daily taking place around him." As we look at the geography of *Persuasion*, we will see how this novel portrays landscape and the heroine differently than either More or Scott do. In a new approach, Austen takes Anne beyond simply "knowing her place" in the world as a woman toward feeling free to go beyond those narrow constraints.

In her last completed novel, Austen begins to push beyond the kind of landscape that More has previously used to express her reluctant position that women should stay where they are—the kind of landscape which moves to the coast and beyond. Anne Elliot is forced to contemplate what it is like to have "a beloved home made over to others" (47). The garden does not belong to her anymore, and she can only survey these former "home scenes" with the permission of the new residents, the Crofts. In a very real way, the heroine of this novel has lost her heritage, unlike the heroine of *Mansfield Park*, who reclaims the proper heritage for everyone, including herself. Fanny knows she belongs to Mansfield Park, but Anne Elliot no longer belongs to Kellynch.

So how does Anne find her *self* now that others occupy Kellynch? Anne finds her *self* in a sensitive connection with her landscape—a landscape that is more than her ancestral home at Kellynch. It is a landscape through which she can read her deepest feelings in the present and yet understand her past. It is a landscape containing a deep cultural impression and possibly something that goes beyond culture. It is an evolutionary landscape, one where a person's response to its beauty is rooted deeply in its functionality and its survival possibilities.

Anne was "forced into prudence in her youth, [but] she learned romance as she grew older—the natural sequel to an unnatural beginning" (30). Psychologists today have frequently connected women with refuges, safety, and small spaces, but Anne finds herself straining against these boundaries.[1] Her refuge—home or hedgerow—has not really benefited her. She does not find much comfort in the social and financial security that she is urged to preserve by her older friend and mother-substitute, Lady Russell. Anne has actually stagnated in her refuge because she followed Lady Russell's advice to preserve the status quo rather than marry a sailor with uncertain prospects.

Unfortunately, Lady Russell has not been the best parental figure for Anne in her attempts to deal with life and landscape. Later in the novel, the reader notices that, elegant though Lady Russell may be, she is too short-sighted and cannot see beyond the window curtains upon which she chooses to focus, rather than recognize Captain Wentworth. At the end of the novel, Anne realizes that she herself must find a new way of viewing her landscape and the future. However, at the beginning of the novel, Anne has only a vague awareness that Lady Russell's advice has not made her happy.

After the Crofts lease Kellynch, Anne moves to Uppercross Cottage, home of her sister, Mary, and finds some new life for herself, although the "small spaces" there seem to be only a temporary cure from her previous stagnation at Kellynch. In Lyme

---

[1] See Erik Erikson's study of attitudes to space ("Womanhood and the Inner Space," *Identity: Youth and Crisis*. NY: Norton, 1968), as well as the works of T. J. Cottle (*Perceiving Time: A Psychological Investigation with Men and Women*. NY: John Wiley and Sons, 1976) and Aharon Kellerman (*Time, Space and Society: Geographical Societal Perspectives*. Boston: Kluwer Academic Publishers, 1989) for a more complete explanation.

she awakens to even greater possibilities. It is as though change is necessary for Anne's happiness. When E. M. Forster writes that in *Sanditon*, "topography comes to the front and is screwed much deeper than usual into the story" (*Abinger Harvest* 154), he makes an astute observation which applies to *Persuasion* as well. While we read this novel as geographers, we can continue to use Appleton's prospect/refuge theory as a means of deepening our understanding of the landscape of *Persuasion*.

But in addition to seeing with the eyes of a geographer, we can also add the dimension of time to this landscape. Gerard Genette suggests that the structure of a literary work is greatly affected by the idea of landscape as a palimpsest of past landscapes. Both the theories of Appleton and Genette help to illuminate a reading of *Persuasion* as a novel where the aesthetics of geography deeply affect the way we interpret the plot. Genette writes that places are active and penetrate the texture of the novel, "ceaselessly recalled, reintegrated, reinvested, always present all at once, and therefore made absent by their very omnipresence" (220). In order to show how Austen's landscapes and heroines contrast with those of male writers, we will turn to Scott's *The Heart of Midlothian* to see how a contemporary male novelist deals with these important aspects in his novel. But first, we examine Hannah More's observation that women have different ways of viewing landscape than do their male counterparts, basically because of how they find themselves stationed most frequently within the land—or sea—scape. When Anne explains to Captain Harville that women "love" differently than men, she struggles with a position with which More has resigned herself, when Anne says of the feelings of women for men:

> We certainly do not forget you, so soon as you forget us. It is, perhaps, our fate rather than our merit. We cannot help ourselves. We live at home, quiet, confined, and our feelings prey upon us. You are forced on exertion. You have always a profession, pursuits, business of some sort or other, to take you back into the world immediately, and continual occupation and change soon weaken impression. (232)[2]

It is worth noting in this passage that the subject is passive, but the man is "forced" into a position that "helps" him; he cannot help himself either. Austen draws attention to the external social forces (not the internal character of a person) that shape gender, and therefore people's lives. The persistence of impressions acts as a palimpsest, as desire and love replace history and the domestic sphere replaces the public sphere.

Both Austen and More seem ambivalent about what they perceive as greater strength—of memory (in Austen) and desire (in More) on the part of women. More, again in her *Strictures*, writes:

> Woman in the career of genius, is the Atalanta,[3] who will risk losing the race by running out of her road to pick up the golden apple; while her male competitor, without, perhaps, possessing greater natural strength or swiftness, will more certainly attain his object, by

---

[2] Not only is Anne echoing More but soon after the publication of *Persuasion*, Byron's sentiments reiterate Anne's feelings:
   Man's love is of man's life, a thing apart,
   'Tis woman's whole existence. ("Don Juan" c. I st. 194)

[3] Atalanta is a mythical young woman. She offered to marry the man who could beat her in a race. Being distracted by the apples, she lost and married the man who won the race, Hippomenes.

being less exposed to be seductions of *extraneous beauty, and will win the race by despising* the bait. [italics mine] (27)

This "extraneous beauty" I believe is found in the landscape; it lies in those natural features to which women are exposed in a limited range, and which, when allowed to run the race, they appreciate all the more. As More writes about woman's prospect from the garden, it *is* more limited than that of a man. And here, where woman and man have the same prospect, she chooses to go where she cannot "win." Because they have been forced by society to stay in one prescribed setting, women have become exceedingly attentive to the smallest nuances of that limited landscape. Have women been conditioned culturally to be more sensitive to emotions and external beauty (either the apple or the landscape) than men? Certainly they have when their own well-being depends upon this conditioning. And if women are "seduced" by scenes on the side of the road, is that their fate, or their merit—or—are women just running a different race? Maybe it is all three.

Austen shows Anne Elliot and Frederick Wentworth relating differently to landscape. Anne views refuges, prospects, and hazards, and yet she extends her vision of the landscape to share the masculine freedom of Wentworth. As Gilbert and Gubar have noted:

> the landscapes she encounters function as a kind of psychic geography of her development so that, when the withered hedgerows and tawny autumnal meadows are replaced by the invigorating breezes and flowing tides of Lyme, we are hardly surprised that Anne's bloom is restored. (178)

More remains ambivalent concerning woman's position in the landscape, urging women to maintain their narrow prospect in the garden, and yet, admitting that women naturally will take the bait of the golden apple lying off the path. Recognizing the educational disadvantages of women, Anne tells Captain Harville, "Men have had every advantage of us in telling their own story. Education has been theirs in so much higher a degree; the pen has been in their hands. I will not allow books to prove any thing" (234). This statement takes Anne (and Austen) beyond More's conventional notions of how women should behave.[4] Anne's awareness of the landscape, far from seducing her by the "exposure to extraneous beauty," has helped her move from a stifling refuge in the garden of Kellynch to a larger one. In the case of Kellynch, a refuge can become a trap.[5] She has broken through that

---

[4] Feminist critics, in recent years have puzzled over how to place Austen in relation to other women writers of her time. Marilyn Butler places her in the Tory proto-feminist tradition. Claudia Johnson views what she calls Austen's political silence as a means of subtly "dismantling" anti-Jacobin "myths" (xxv), while she finds More's works to "advance the strictest programs for female subordination and the most repressive standards of female propriety" (16). However, Johnson concedes that "the codes employed by the two opposing camps are not always so discrete and mutually exclusive" (xxii). I place myself somewhere between Butler and Johnson. I agree that Austen allows her female characters freedom beyond that conceived of by More, but Austen's nationalist stance in *Emma* and *Persuasion* does not seem to "dismantle anti-Jacobin myths."

[5] Johnson's chapter on *Persuasion*, "The 'Unfeudal Tone of the Present Day'" (*Jane Austen: Women, Politics, and the Novel*. Chicago: U of Chicago P, 1988), comments on Austen's position: "By

rational world of Mansfield Park into what Ellen Moers has called an "oceanic feeling" (260) for the landscape. Admittedly, Anne has not achieved this "oceanic feeling" without the help of a man. (Is the ocean a kind of road here for the "men-of-war" to carry culture to the colonies?) "She gloried in being a sailor's wife, but she must pay the tax of quick alarm for belonging to that profession" (252). She will no doubt go to sea with her husband, as Mrs. Croft has done, and experience the "challenges and threats" that balance out and make a refuge all the more valuable.[6]

***

Aesthetic Geography, Women, and *Persuasion*

As has been noted in previous chapters, Appleton suggests that pleasurable sensations in the experience of the landscape are related to environmental conditions favorable to biological survival (vii), and his concept of prospect/refuge analyzes the landscape in terms of its "strategic appraisal as potential habitat" (vii). He also sees expression and perception as part of a single relationship with the behavior of the perceiver being influenced by the environment.

Habitat theory then is the ability of a place to satisfy biological needs, and prospect/refuge theory is "the ability to see without being seen [which] is conducive to the exploitation of environmental conditions favourable to biological survival and is therefore a source of pleasure" (270). The inhabitant gravitates towards a good place to hide and a good place from which to see. Additionally, the aesthetic satisfaction is related to the fact that the landscape favors the physical survival of the individual. Appleton's interests lie not so much in one's domination of the landscape as in one's coexistence with it. Appleton emphasizes "coexistence"; however, it is important to note that Patricia Spacks, author of *The Female Imagination*, comments that "the close connection between self-control and concealment for a woman" is particularly important (82). She views this connection as a theme of many eighteenth- and nineteenth-century novels, noting that a woman's manners should *conceal* her cleverness, certainly a trait recognizable in Anne Elliot. So self-control and concealment allow the self to perceive the landscape as a habitat and in so doing brings itself into being as an inhabitor.

So far, we have seen this habitat theory as it applies to Austen's work as early as the bower in "Catharine,—or The Bower" and later in Fanny's love of Mansfield

---

linking women's confinement within changeless neighborhoods to the strength and longevity of their feelings, she develops this tradition with particular emphasis on women's problems" (159). This remark I feel expresses what Austen is trying to do in order to highlight the difficulties of her heroines.

[6] Gary Kelly in "Jane Austen, Romantic Feminism, and Civil Society" (*Jane Austen and Discourses of Feminism*, ed. Devoney Looser. NY: St. Martin's, 1995), sees Austen (and More) as mediating between subject, domesticity, and the state, following a period of social and political upheaval. According to Kelly, More saw women as those who were "called to heroic defense of the 'national' culture, identity, and destiny within and from the ideological and cultural bastion of the home" (22). In *Persuasion* Kelly claims that Austen sees naval society as the answer to Britain's need for renewal and stabilization. Monica Cohen, as well, discusses the relation between domesticity and the professionalism of the navy in "Persuading the Navy Home: Austen and Married Women's Professional Property" in *Novel* 29 (1996): 346-366.

Park. What originally must have related these refuges directly to safety can make them aesthetically attractive in fiction. In the "Hedgerow Chapter" (Chapter 10) of *Persuasion*, Austen describes an outstanding prospect/refuge scene for the heroine, which allows her both to position herself for learning information important to her well-being and also to conceal herself safely.

But first, Anne needs to leave a "refuge" that no longer "works" as a place for her to grow as a woman. Initially she is very reluctant to change space or nature. What are the advantages to Anne's living at Kellynch-hall? Lady Russell thinks Anne has become too reclusive. "Anne had been too little from home, too little seen. Her spirits were not high. A larger society would improve them" (15). Anne herself thinks that "seeing the lawns and groves of Kellynch" (14) might be enough for her. According to the opportunistic, fortune-hunting friend of Sir Walter, Mrs. Clay, only the men who can live on their own property "without the torment of trying for more" stay healthy and young-looking (21). Of course, she says this to flatter Sir Walter, but she is comparing his position as landholder to that of the sailor. "The sea is no beautifier," says Mrs. Clay (20). But she is wrong, and, since both she and Sir Walter are discussing the merits of superficial good-looks over the ill-effects of an active outdoors life, the reader may wonder whether staying put on the estate forever is really beneficial to anyone, certainly a very different notion from the one established in *Mansfield Park*. Inactivity on the estate may preserve a person's youthful looks, but the rigors of the sea allow a person to engage life more completely.

Anne learns to adapt only when she is forced to do so. For the first third of the novel, she seeks out a refuge in her landscape. If she cannot continue at Kellynch, then Uppercross Cottage will be her home. If she does go walking out-of-doors, she takes care not to be exposed to the view of others. She uses any reason she can to stay in the cottage and avoids going abroad. When all the Musgroves and Captain Wentworth go for a walk toward Winthrop, "she would have staid at home; but for some feelings of interest and curiosity" (84). Just the three-mile move from Kellynch to Uppercross has stimulated her at least a little.

The "Hedgerow Chapter" serves to demonstrate how a certain kind of landscape, and positioning of the heroine in it, can provide the prospect and the refuge she needs. One way to contrast how a male writer handles the same prospect/refuge is to refer to William Wordsworth. His "Lucy" poems find Lucy dying and becoming one with the landscape—something that might have happened to Anne if she had been allowed to mope away in the garden at Kellynch. Another of Wordsworth's poems, "Nutting," shows the male prospector in an autumnal landscape very similar to that which Austen describes in *Persuasion*. Both "Nutting" and the Hedgerow Chapter offer chances to hide and to seek, but these refuges turn out very differently depending on the gender of the character focalizer of the landscape. Interestingly enough, what Anne and the boy going nutting have in common is that, in starting out, both propose to remain indifferent to the landscape, and yet neither can remain detached.

The narrator as a boy thinks he knows what he is about; he is "fearless of a rival" and looks for the unspoiled refuge with the rather vague idea of "forcing [his] way" (l.16). Anne, on the other hand, does not want to be in the way. She is trying to avoid her rival, Louisa Musgrove, as well as Frederick Wentworth, her former lover. In both cases, Anne and the boy find their spot, but in the boy's situation, what he thought was a refuge—some "virgin scene" which he might dominate (in fact, "mercilessly ravage")—shifts. He has forfeited his ability to hide and his ability to coexist with his environment.

> ... Then up I rose,
> And dragged to earth both branch and bough, with crash
> And merciless ravage: and the shady nook
> Of hazels, and the green and mossy bower,
> Deformed and sullied, patiently gave up
> Their quiet being: and, unless I now
> Confound my present feelings with the past:
> Ere from the mutilated bower I turned
> Exulting, rich beyond the wealth of kings,
> I felt a sense of pain when I beheld
> The silent trees, and saw the intruding sky.—
> Then, dearest Maiden, move along these shades
> In gentleness of heart; with gentle hand
> Touch—for there is a spirit in the woods. (43-56)

Anne is trying to hide in the hedgerow; she is avoiding being seen, not intending to seek. And yet, her refuge becomes an unexpected prospect. The scene in Wordsworth's poem shows the boy's nascent sexual impulses, combined with his violently destructive response to the landscape. Of course, while Anne's experience is distilled into five minutes, in "Nutting," the poet/boy-grown-into-manhood is uncertain about when he felt shame for what he has mutilated in the landscape—"Unless I now/ Confound my present feelings with the past ... I felt a sense of pain when I beheld/ The silent trees" (ll.48-9, 52-3). But at the time, the boy exults over basically raping the landscape that should have served as a refuge, only to realize that he has destroyed the very place that would have been a safe haven for him. "Haymaker and Sleeping Girl" (1785) by Gainsborough illustrates a similar gaze, with the young woman asleep, unaware of the young man looking down on her as she is slumped against a fence in the natural setting. He does not seem to be thinking of violating her, yet he is definitely the spectator in control of the gaze, and the woman is the one being gazed upon without her knowledge or permission. The spectators in the Wordsworth poem and the Gainsborough painting illustrate a much different position for a woman than the position in which Austen places Anne.

Anne finds that, even without her willing it, her refuge becomes a prospect. She chooses the hedgerow as a place to stay still, similar to the way Fanny sits on a bench at the edge of the wilderness—to remain quiet and out of the social mainstream until her companions are ready to walk back. But in Anne's respect for her refuge, she finds that her position in it acts as a prospect, where she learns her deepest feelings as she responds to the beauty rooted in the scene, so unlike Wordsworth's boy's approach to the refuge scene. She overhears Wentworth and Louisa without their detecting her presence. And instead of feeling a final sense of helplessness and shame, she begins to experience the power of knowledge—knowledge (not without embarrassment) that Wentworth still cares about her and knowledge that he knows she has turned down another suitor after him. This newly found knowledge, discovered in this prospect, gives her the power to act, even as she is oppressed.

90 *Prospect and Refuge in the Landscape of Jane Austen*

Figure 6.1 Thomas Gainsborough, "Haymaker and Sleeping Girl." Courtesy of Museum of Fine Arts, Boston. M. Theresa B. Hopkins Fund and Seth K. Sweetser Fund. 53.2553.

A sense exists in both these scenes that the boy and Wentworth do not take their environment seriously enough. The boy finds his spot to gather nuts fascinating for the simple reason that it is untouched. He toys with his environment and then destroys it. What Anne overhears in the hedgerow is also masculine toying with the environment—Wentworth too finds a hazelnut but, with a kind of ironic distance, seems to need to separate himself from nature by making up a metaphor:

> "Here is a nut," said he, catching one down from an upper bough. "To exemplify,—a beautiful glossy nut which blessed with original strength, has outlived all the storms of autumn. Not a puncture, not a weak spot any where.—This nut," he continued, with playful solemnity,—"while so many of its brethren have fallen and been trodden under foot, is still in possession of all the happiness that a hazel-nut can be supposed capable of." (88)

Like the boy, Wentworth wants to control his environment. The ironic distancing of himself from the environment around him through personification positions him in a way that never occurs to Anne with her deep, more serious, emotional attachment to nature. Wentworth (and the boy) might be associated with culture (as Ortner defines it: human consciousness by which "humanity attempts to assert control over nature" [72]). Anne's sense of power asserts its superiority over Wentworth's because, as a woman, she resides on the edge of nature and culture, helping to convert one to the other. She has the advantage of combining the subject and object of power.

Louisa is that "nut," as strong in mind as the nut is in its physical capabilities. But Wentworth is being playful here, and later the reader may realize, he has been rather simplistic as well. Louisa is foolishly hard-headed, and it is Anne who exhibits the best qualities of the hazelnut. Wentworth is also hazarding his chances with Anne (although he is not aware of it) by his thoughtless playfulness. Similarly, the boy ruins his chances of a pleasurable and safe refuge by virtually raping the setting as though it was some virginal yet inanimate girl.

Anne accepted the refuge for what it was—"a nice seat ... in the hedgerow, in which she had no doubt of there being—in some spot or other" (87). "A bush of low rambling holly protected her" (88). In neither trying to dominate nor submit to the landscape, Anne, to her surprise, discovers that she can learn a great deal from the landscape that she may later use to her benefit (and perhaps even for her survival). As the next generation of heroines, such as Charlotte Brontë's Lucy Snowe of *Villette*, find out, women inadvertently and deliberately find that voyeurism is a primary way to gain power—that prospect from hiding on the edge of the wood.

Appleton would probably describe the Hedgerow Chapter as a scene greatly dependent upon refuge imagery. The hedgerow is located on "the brow of the hill" (86), and "commanded a full view" (85) of Winthrop, but there is something distinctly unsatisfactory about this prospect: "Winthrop, without beauty and without dignity, was stretched before them; an indifferent house, standing low, and hemmed in by the barns and buildings of a farm-yard" (85). If the prospect here had been more absorbing, then possibly Anne would not have searched out a refuge to begin with.

But what happens when the female characters stray from the zone of safety? A landscape of exposure becomes evident as soon as the characters in *Persuasion* go to Lyme and, as might be expected, impetuous Louisa is the one who ignores this hazard. The Cobb retains all the aspects which Appleton describes as a zone of exposure, hazardous in every way to the woman who does not take heed of the dangers. Of course, we all know the story of Captain Wentworth reluctantly "jumping" Louisa Musgrove down the slick Granny's Teeth, narrow steps proceeding down from the top level of the seawall called the Cobb that protrudes into the English Channel at Lyme Regis. Virtually no shelter or refuge exists there, neither is there any protected prospect; the seawall juts out into the water, exposed as far as the Lias cliffs on the distant shore. Anne understands the danger into which Louisa is placing herself when she insists on jumping the steps, and although Anne cannot stop her, she does have more presence of mind than any others at the scene to direct the rescue when Louisa falls and is finally taken to Captain Harville's house near the Cobb.

Not only does Anne know how to respect a landscape of exposure and handle herself well in it, but also she appreciates the vitality of this seascape. Being present in this open environment revitalizes Anne. Anne calls forth a landscape, and it calls her forth; she becomes a true inhabitor of this landscape, with all the power and confidence that this entails. Anne and her party "soon found themselves on the sea shore, and lingering only, as all must linger and gaze on a first return to the sea, who ever deserve to look on it at all" (96). Her emotions are more closely attuned to the landscape, yet again she seeks neither to dominate nor to submit to it. Anne learns from the landscape and tries to teach the overly sentimental Captain Benwick about the dangers of poetry. She sees the deeper geology of the landscape that affects the "proportions and limits" (116) of the mind more than the emotionality of poetry. She suggests for him a good dose of "our best moralists" to "rouse and fortify the mind by the highest precepts" (101). And even later, she muses that Wentworth ought to realize by now that "firmness of character" should have "proportions and limits" as well.

"Proportions and limits" of the mind relate to the landscape well. Appleton's theory that response to the landscape involves a prior concept of beauty based upon functionality applies here. Functionality is basically ignored when scenes of nature artificially combine with poetry to induce a heightened state of sorrow. Those scenes that Benwick used to depress himself into useless poetic misery were misuses of a landscape. Benwick's over-sentimentalizing of Nature may have seemed charming to some but did not really function as a means of survival. Anne, however, learned from the environment. She found signs in the landscape that became favorable to her emotional survival. And so it is not at all surprising that she found "the bloom and freshness of youth restored by the fine wind which had been blowing on her complexion, and by the animation of eye which it had also produced" (104). Both her cousin William Elliot and Frederick Wentworth noticed as well.

The landscape around Lyme which revitalizes Anne, Gilbert and Gubar call "psychic geography" and suggest naval life as a possible escape for Anne from other more stifling and artificial landscape such as that of Bath. The oceanic feeling here has to do with space, prospect, and a sense of getting out of that narrow kitchen garden. Walking around the countryside of Uppercross must have been a liberating feeling for a woman who expected always to have the narrow view of Hannah More's garden. More herself tries to convince women:

> Is it not then more wise as well as more honourable to move contentedly in the plain path which Providence has obviously marked out to the sex, and in which custom has for the most part rationally confirmed them rather than to stray awkwardly, unbecomingly, and unsuccessfully in a forbidden road? to be the lawful possessors of a lesser domestic territory, rather than the turbulent usurpers of a wider foreign empire? (*Strictures* 22)

If Anne Elliot were being completely honest, she would recognize and admit the appeal of that forbidden road to the wider foreign empire, and she is not rash, awkward, or unbecoming. Maybe someone such as Mrs. Croft has found a way for women to take their "lesser domestic" duties to sea—to join the "men-of-war" on what Hannah More sees as a "forbidden road."

But how to get there and still maintain what Jane Austen considered the responsible feminine ties with society? The Crofts provide the answer to this question. They seem to have what Austen would consider the right relation to the landscape (and I include seascape here as well). Anne finds she could easily do worse than to follow their example. In the end, Anne seeks to become a more elegant version of Mrs. Croft. Mrs. Croft lacks Anne's "elegance of mind" (5). This "elegance," according to the *Oxford English Dictionary*, encompasses a "grace of form" (as the result of art or culture) and a "grace of physical movement" as well. So Anne eventually combines the emotional and even biological survival techniques exhibited by Mrs. Croft, but Anne's character possesses an artistic grace which makes her even more pleasing. And so, we are back to Appleton and the combination of aesthetic satisfaction and favorable survival factors in a landscape and the women who, in this case, interact with the natural environment.

Anne recognizes a deeper, more functional foundation in the landscape than that of artistic pleasure. Captain and Mrs. Croft exemplify a relation to their environment that functions quite well. Sir Walter presumes that living at Kellynch must be the height of luxury for the Crofts, and yet they seem not to be overawed by the place at all. All of Sir Walter's mirrors baffle Captain Croft, and the Crofts must learn to adapt to the smoke that comes down the chimney when the wind is blowing a certain way. But Mrs. Croft makes it clear though that the best refuge is a ship: "I know nothing superior to the accommodations of a man of war. I declare I have not a comfort or an indulgence about me even at Kellynch-hall ... beyond what I always had in most of the ships I have lived in" (69). Although her brother, Captain Wentworth, expresses great reluctance to have women aboard his ship, Mrs. Croft has a more realistic view of women and tells him, "But I hate to hear you talking so, like a fine gentleman, and as if women were all fine ladies, instead of rational creatures. We none of us expect to be in smooth water all our days" (70).

This love of the open spaces (which might remind them of the life at sea) causes the Crofts to spend a good deal of their time at Kellynch outdoors "interesting themselves in their new possessions, their grass, and their sheep" (73). They know how to adapt and are equally at ease on land and at sea. And they seem to treat the open land as they would the open sea, sailing around in their gig. Their land travels around the countryside seem very much like their sea voyages might be like. Captain Wentworth says:

> What glorious weather for the Admiral and my sister! They meant to take a long drive this morning; perhaps we may hail them from some of these hills. They talked of coming into this side of the country. I wonder whereabouts they will upset to-day. Oh! it does happen very often, I assure you—but my sister makes nothing of it—she would as lieve be tossed out as not. (84)

Mrs. Croft even tugs on the reins to keep them on course. The reader can picture her taking the same delight in the dangers of sailing. She—and Anne, eventually—recognize the naval life as a means by which a woman can stay within proper social boundaries and yet push beyond those boundaries into "geographical pockets of excess" from which women are normally excluded.[7]

Also naval life seems to have that fine functional balance of prospect and refuge with just enough hazards to make life interesting. The ship has a high refuge value, and the Crofts' accommodations on land take on that same value. They are always "strategically appraising" the landscape as "potential habitat," to use Appleton's terms. When they feel a need for refuge, they merely explain it this way:

> [we] shut [ourselves] into [our] lodgings, and draw in our chairs, and are as snug as if we were at Kellynch, ay, or as we used to be even at North Yarmouth and Deal. We do not like our lodgings here the worse, I can tell you, for putting us in mind of those we first had at North Yarmouth. The wind blows through one of the cupboards just in the same way. (170)

What a wonderful image of a present refuge and all the other refuges from the past that they remember so well.

Yet there is a practicality with the way Captain and Mrs. Croft deal with prospects and refuges which appears deeper and more real than any poetic or artistic artificial landscapes can be. Austen makes clear how she values a functional approach (proportions and limits) to the scene more than she does any whimsical poetic license. Captain Croft criticizes a picture of a boat, seen in a shop window, and, not for its artistic merit, but for its lack of practicality.

> What queer fellows your fine painters must be, to think that any body would venture their lives in such a shapeless old cockleshell as that. And yet, here are two gentlemen stuck up in it mightily at their ease, and looking around them at the rocks and mountains, as if they were not to be upset the next moment, which they certainly must be. (169)

Constable suggests that a painting pleases by reminding, not deceiving. Just as when Anne condemns Benwick's use of poetry as a way of unrealistically distorting his emotions, Austen condemns painting of scenery that is not truthful both metaphorically and psychologically. A ship in a painting can stand for something else, but it still must look like an actual ship. Plausible psychological motivations

---

[7] George Levine, in describing the Victorian landscape, discusses an English countryside from which society would seem to ban extremes. Therefore, he thinks novelists tend to establish "geographical pockets of excess" elsewhere (maybe in a foreign country—France or Italy is a popular choice). Drownings (as in Charlotte Bronte's *Villette*) suggest "another 'place' in the realist landscape for the monstrous possibilities that society and the English countryside would seem to exclude" (*The Realistic Imagination* 206).

for characters' actions—in painting or novel—are as important for Austen as an intriguing, but faulty, metaphor. Croft shows that he (and Mrs. Croft, as well) knows a real refuge and recognizes real hazards as well, even as they welcome the challenge of them.

***

Layers of Landscape and Time

Appleton's aesthetic geographical ways of viewing the artistic landscape can be enriched by the addition of Genette's way of regarding symbolism as a figure, or gap, between poetic language and what he calls ordinary language. How a reader— or character—can fill in this "gap" might become the bridge Appleton describes between the requirement of biological survival and the pleasurable sensations derived from contemplating landscape. In Genette's narratology, the figure supplies a surplus of meaning. For instance, a writer chooses to use "sail" to indicate "ship"—a part for the whole, and yet, because he uses "sail" instead of "hull," the hiatus between the two has quite a different meaning. Although Genette does not explain the social implications of his poetic language, necessarily the choice of sign and the surplus of meaning it might have for any given member of society would involve the sign and surplus with the ideologies of a society. For instance, Captain Croft finds it impossible to fill in the gap between the "cockleshell" of a boat in the painting he sees and his own notion of a real boat which is constructed actually to stay afloat, because he sees the "figure" as implausible.

The poetic landscape created by a writer, according to Genette, is a palimpsest— a parchment written upon several times before with the previous texts only imperfectly erased. Genette sees both time and place as palimpsests, the characters having the ability to know the essence of a moment or place through other moments or places, which have some but not all qualities in common. (This term, "palimpsest" has been used elsewhere in this study to show basically what lies behind and within some of the landscapes, maybe only partially evident to the reader—and character, nevertheless significantly adding to the complexity of the scene.) Genette sees metaphor as a necessary instrument of recovery of the psychological experience of memory. The best Anne can hope for when she discovers that her father is renting Kellynch is to know that her former lover, the brother of Mrs. Croft, might walk where she is walking now. "As she walked along a favourite grove," she realizes that "a few months more, and *he*, perhaps, may be walking here" (25). The palimpsest of her still-beloved Captain Wentworth having walked with her in these groves before and possibly walking there in the future makes Kellynch a valuable refuge for her. As she walks where he walked/will walk, she can in a sense *be him* in this landscape—insert herself into the historical palimpsest *as* Wentworth.[8]

---

[8] For another instance of Austen making a given identity something someone else can occupy by inhabiting the same space in the same way, the reader might examine the function of theater in *Mansfield Park*, where the transformation of identity into role enables people to be "more themselves" (e.g., Mary Crawford to express her love for Edmund, Henry to reveal his desire for women, Maria to reveal that she is as much a victim of a flattering man as Agatha in *Lovers' Vow*s).

But all is memory, and she attempts to "clothe her imagination, her memory, her ideas in as much Uppercross as possible" (43). The landscape is clothing for the character, a new refuge, however ill-fitting. Not only does the person "own" the clothing of the landscape, there is also a mutuality here of the landscape "owning" people as well, as when her home, the "groves and prospects ... own other eyes and limbs" (47-48). Anne even sees herself as a kind of landscape and one which has the quality of a palimpsest, when she notices Frederick Wentworth "observing her altered features, perhaps, trying to trace in them the ruins of the face which had once charmed him" (72). Finally, Anne is forced to learn to adapt to a new landscape. She must leave her refuge, which did not seem to be really good for her anyway. But she does so reluctantly. "It would be most right, and most wise, and therefore, must involve least suffering, to go with the others" (33)

As Anne gains new insight into emotions, her sense of the landscape continues to affect the course of her relationship with Wentworth. But so far, the landscape with which Anne has had to interact has been close to home and emotionally similar to the garden scene of Hannah More's. Although Ellen Moers identifies certain places beneficial to women as "open lands, harsh and upswelling, high-lying and undulating, vegetated with crimped heather or wind-swept grasses, cut with ravines and declivities and twisting lanes" (262), these features have a great deal of similarity to the seascape Anne encounters at Lyme Regis. Moers sees these outdoor scenes as a means of feminine self-discovery and self-assertion. The Brontë moors and the Cather plains seem to have a kind of mystic "oceanic feeling" to them which, even though the women there are land-bound, generates in them a "sense of selflessness and release from the flesh" (260), rather like going to sea.

Anne has her first experience with this kind of landscape when she travels to Lyme. The "psychic" topography of Lyme appears to fit very well into prospect/refuge theory, as well as appearing as a palimpsest of layered landscapes. The reader must remember that it is a man who transports Anne to Lyme. Wentworth's "description of the fine country about Lyme [was] so feelingly attended to by the party" (94) that of course they all had to see it. But as Anne is able to use the information she gleaned in the hedgerow to her advantage, she also learns much from Lyme.

Lyme embodies the ideal balance of prospect and refuge formed by geological layers. The Cobb has a history far more significant than the bathing machine season's superficiality, "its old wonders and new improvements, with the very beautiful line of cliffs stretching out to the east of the town" (95).[9] Anne sees "extensive sweeps of country, and still more its sweet retired bay, backed by dark cliffs, where fragments of low rock among the sands make it the happiest spot for watching the flow of the tide, for sitting in unwearied contemplation" (95). The blue Lias cliffs, visible from both the Cobb and the Charmouth fields near Lyme, are composed of limestone and a series of ancient rocks containing many fossils. What

---

[9] In fact today, Lyme Regis is frequently called the center of the Jurassic Coast. During Jane Austen's lifetime, Mary Anning, who lived in Lyme Regis, "helped discover the first complete ichthyosaur specimen to come to the attention of London's scientific community" (11), according to an article in *The New York Times* (July 11, 2004). "She blazed a trail for many of the more famous scientists who later combed these cliffs" (11).

the Lyme landscape has in common with the Cather prairies and the Brontë moors involves not close physical resemblance so much as an ability to psychically stimulate the heroine's mind toward a new sense of freedom and control of her environment. Oddly enough, it is a landscape with a history, yet not bounded by these events. The Lyme landscape provides a way for Anne to escape her concrete circumstances.

If this balance of prospect/refuge scenery is not enough to inspire the viewer, she still has

> the woody variety of the cheerful village of Up Lyme, and above all, Pinny, with its green chasms between romantic rocks, where the scattered forest trees and orchards of luxuriant growth declare that many a generation must have passed away since the first partial falling of the cliff prepared the ground for such a state. (*Persuasion* 96)

The old pier is of "unknown date." The palimpsest here has a balance of natural history (a way to evade written history). The scene is described as one which "must be visited again and again, to make the worth of Lyme understood" (96). The natural history of the Lyme landscape (as that of other landscapes which allow women to thrive—on prairie or moor) provides a location for the heroine to exist on the edge of the wood (nature) and confront some of the contradictions and inequalities of society and culture (the clearing).[10]

Many kinds of "memory" are involved—the novelist's, the character's and the culture's. The poetic landscape can therefore bring together multiple sensations separated by time. Landscapes of other moments in life are carried along with the characters (and authors) in the present landscape—archeology suggesting the layering of moments in a novelistic landscape. Austen's scene on the walk to Winthrop provides another good example of layering:

> Her pleasure in the walk must arise from the exercise and the day, from the view of the last smiles of the year upon the tawny leaves and withered hedges, and from repeating to herself some few of the thousand poetical descriptions extant of autumn, that season of peculiar and inexhaustible influence on the mind of taste and tenderness, that season which has drawn from every poet, worthy of being read, some attempt at description, or some line of feeling. (84)

This passage demonstrates how Genette's idea of palimpsest, which he demonstrates using Proust, might work in Austen.

***

"Images of Felicitous Space"

Both Appleton and Genette call attention to our perception of landscape from the perspective of aesthetic geography (we are attracted, sometimes subconsciously, to

---

[10] Two metaphors come to mind as Anne sees the sea and Wentworth together. Could the sea be a way of seeing Wentworth as Pemberley is a way of seeing Darcy? They seem to be similar recognition scenes.

locations which we feel will help us survive) and from the perspective of literary criticism (many tissues of consciousness affect the meaning of landscape). Other critics, especially philosophers, have addressed the subject of space also. In *The Poetics of Space*, Bachelard examines what he calls "quite simple images of felicitous space" (xxxi). Bachelard discusses the sheltered being giving perceptible limits to her shelter and daydreams as a synthesis of "immemorial and recollected memories." He mentions the comfort human beings receive by reliving memories of protection, and the physical pleasure of withdrawing into corners. Bachelard brings together the ideas of space both as refuge and as palimpsest. In *Persuasion*, Austen clearly shows Lyme Regis as such a place for Anne. The area has memories that go deep into her psyche. She instinctively recognizes the fields and seashore as a place with which she feels comfortable, and these feelings lead to greater self-confidence on her part.

Bachelard discusses how psychically invigorating changing landscapes can be for a person; a person not only changes space but also nature. He refers to some space as "intimate immensity:" "to go down into the water, or to wander in the desert, is to change space, and by changing space, by leaving the space of one's usual sensibilities, one enters into communication with a space that is psychically innovating." Bachelard adds, "For we do not change place, we change our nature" (206). All Anne Elliot needs to do is to leave home and discover the "intimate immensity" of the seashore and, later, the water itself.

This brings us back to the concept of liminality ("the betwixt and between moments when people are disposed to feel liberated from the norms of their society" [Hughes 22]). The beach then has an "ill-defined margin ... As a physical threshold, a limen, the beach has been difficult to dominate ... providing the basis for an 'outsider' position" (Shields qtd in Hughes 22).[11] Lyme, its Cobb, and its windswept hills allow Anne, as an outsider, to find her real self in this threshold scene; it is not her ultimate "refuge," but it gives her the courage to find that ultimate refuge: life at sea. There Wentworth's ship will be the "cottage-by-the-wood" with the prospect being the ocean and the intimacy of her marriage to Wentworth.

Austen draws her landscapes without the minute description of later novelists, such as Dickens, but these landscapes provide her heroines with spaces to reflect knowledgeably—even psychically—upon their situations. As Bachelard examines "images of *felicitous space*," he suggests that "topophilia" be used to "seek to determine the human value of the sorts of space that may be grasped, that may be defended against adverse forces, the space we love" (xxxi). This space is private and to disclose too much about it takes away from that sense of intimacy. Bachelard suggests that too much description of a place is like revealing one's private thoughts to those we do not know well. So Austen's landscapes, as her heroines' physical descriptions, remain unspecified, allowing us as readers to fill in the gap of what we imagine the landscape really is.

---

[11] As we saw earlier, Mieke Bal suggests that a boundary can sometimes be a trap. It may be a trap in the case of Anne, stuck on the edge of Kellynch and unable to bring herself to leave easily. Or the trap may be literally the "man trap" that catches Lucy in "Jack and Alice." But a limen is a more permeable place with room to move around.

***

Scott's Heroine in the Landscape

Nature inspires both Austen and Scott, but as we have seen in the previous discussion of *Persuasion*, Austen prefers to deal with small amounts of relived time, whereas Scott moves directly from on-site perception straight to culture. Austen's goal seems to be that the story of her novel *could* be real; Scott wants us to think that his story *is* real. As a way of further illuminating Austen's treatment of the heroine in the landscape, we will now look at how Scott places his heroine, Jeanie Deans, in the landscape of *The Heart of Midlothian*.

The Heart of Midlothian was written around the same time that Austen was writing *Persuasion*. Frequently regarded as Scott's best novel, *The Heart of Midlothian* deals with landscapes of both England and Scotland following the Edinburgh riots of 1736. The heroine of this novel, Jeanie Deans, from a peasant family with strong patriarchal religious beliefs, spends all of her energies attempting to save her sister, Effie, from being executed for child-murder.

Kenneth Craik, in "Psychological Reflections on Landscape," discusses the layers of influence that surround the on-site impression a viewer has of the landscape. First and closest to the on-site impression is what he terms the psychological sets of viewers. Next come the roles in which they perceive themselves. After that comes personality, followed and backed by the perceivers' cultures. Although all these layers of perception probably influence both Austen and Scott, Austen focuses more on the psychological set and the personality of the observer, and Scott seems less interested in these aspects of perception. Georg Luckàcs praises Scott's ability to prepare readers for a historical personality, pointing out that "this preparation ... is not a personal and psychological one, but objective, social-historical" (38).

Craik's findings on the influence of landscape and the way they relate to Austen and Scott may not be altogether surprising, considering some of the other psychologists' studies concerning gender and space (Erikson, in particular). With a gendered approach to landscape, we are looking not at a biological given, but at a set of responses to culture and the way men and women perceive their gender roles in a particular society at a particular historical time.

Both Anne Elliot and Jeanie Deans occupy mediating positions between nature and culture, but Anne mediates a position that favors herself as a freer and happier woman, whereas the mediating position occupied by Jeanie favors the moral and historical stance of Scott. Jeanie does not learn anything to help her own emotional or intellectual state through her experience in the landscape; Scott basically uses her as an objective mediating device between nature and culture in the English and Scottish landscapes.

Persuasion and *The Heart of Midlothian* are both in a sense elegiac, taking place during a time of historical change. However, Jane Austen, in contrast to Scott, rarely refers to historical events in any of her novels, despite the fact that she had a keen interest in both historical and current affairs. Scott, in his 1831 introduction to *The Fortunes of Nigel*, articulates the idea of a cultural frame for viewing history, much like a frame for viewing a landscape with the "ancient rough and wide manner of a barbarous age" (representing the Scottish culture of the centuries prior to 1700) and the "illumination of increasing or revived learning" (representing England) (xx).

Both Austen and Scott appear concerned with prospects and refuges as well as hazards in the landscape. The prospects, refuges, and hazards in *Persuasion* appear frequently to be more poetic, as well as literal; however, Scott seems more interested in cultural, historical, and moral borders in the landscape, describing the most romantic area of a country being the place where the mountains meet the plains. Walter Scott's narrator teaches his readers through a heroine who is so much a part of the landscape that no clear separation exists between self and environment—she is *in* the landscape but cannot see it. Cosgrove describes the control of the external world that was so important to eighteenth-century thinkers. "For the insider the external world is unmediated by aesthetic conventions and the experience of the insider is denied. Subjectivity belongs to the artist who controls the landscape" (26). Although certainly Austen was an artist, she had an insider's feeling for the landscape, whereas Scott was definitely "the artist who controls the landscape" by remaining outside.

One scene in *The Heart of Midlothian*, in particular, represents the way a male novelist, Scott, uses his heroine in the landscape. St. Leonard's Crags, near the relatively civilized Edinburgh, represents a kind of immoral lawlessness. It is just on the edge of wilderness and considered by many an "ill-reputed district" (149). According to Scott's history of the area, a "fairy boy" had, "among the recesses of these romantic cliffs, found his way into the hidden retreats where the fairies revel in the bowels of the earth" (149). So the old Convenanters were as trapped in their traditions, as Jeanie Deans is in hers as the daughter of a rigid Convenanter. On one side of St. Leonard's, the martyrs of the Convenant faced in the "recesses of mountains, in caverns, and in morasses ... the Enemy of mankind, as in the cities and cultivated fields, they were exposed to those [assaults] of the tyrannical government and their soldiery" (149).

Jeanie is aware of the traditions of this landscape, and, on the present night, only the imminent threat to her sister's life could force her to go to this place. In this landscape, Jeanie feels compelled to meet with a man who seems to be a devil but who turns out to be her sister's lover. The moon begins "to peer forth on the scene with a doubtful, flitting, and solemn light" and Jeanie's fears are declared by the narrator as "too peculiar to her rank and country to remain unnoticed" (148). She is a part of another cultural-historical landscape without unique feelings of her own. The narrator sketches the scene as someone seeing Jeanie in the landscape. We are privy to her thoughts of the landscape, but we already know that they are based on superstitions common to her upbringing. This depiction of Jeanie is Scott's idea of how a brave female representative of eighteenth-century Scottish culture would probably act. But a distance exists here between the mind of the narrator (and Scott) and what is going on in Jeanie's mind. Jeanie is truly a figure in the landscape, one who stands for the most admirable of old Scottish culture, yet one we as readers view objectively as we would an actor on a large stage set. The same is not true with our perception of Anne Elliot; we are in the hedgerow with her. And when Captain Wentworth lifts her large nephew from her back, we realize what has happened as though we are in her mind. In contrast though, here is Jeanie as a figure in the landscape:

> So, like Christiana in the Pilgrim's Progress when traversing with a timid yet resolved step the terrors of the Valley of the Shadow of Death, she glided on by rock and stone, "now in glimmer and now in gloom," as her path lay through moonlight or shadow. (150)

Jeanie is like Christiana and stands in this hazardous landscape as the firm upholder of her father's morality. Anne Elliot does not act as a representative of a culture (and certainly does not represent her father's morality) or become like a character from a book; "she was only Anne."

Although in both *Persuasion* and *The Heart of Midlothian*, the authors treat the moral aspects of nature, Austen's treatment of nature and the landscape is more deeply emotional and less self-conscious than Scott's treatment. What Anne learns from her landscape consists of a complicated network of memories from her personal and literary past. But as we have seen, she distrusts the literary aspect of the landscape for its ability to stir up artificial emotions, and Austen gives her heroine the authority to show Benwick the "right" way of looking at landscape.

Scott's treatment of the environment might be labeled as more distancing—the Claude glass images of the Highlands. Scott appears to be following Addison's tenet from a 1712 *Spectator* essay: "We find the works of nature still more pleasant the more they resemble those of art." In *The Heart of Midlothian* Scott uses landscape as metaphor for political history and legalistic morality. His sense of time in the landscape is linear—the past, present, and future of each scene revealed. His landscape is very much a public one, well-known to many readers, and he appears eager to succeed in a public purpose—convincing readers to see and understand what has gone on until the present. To this end, he uses a kind of spatial analogy that resembles an edge-of-the-woods effect as a border between two kinds of landscape (although not seamless in that the border is one which conceals a fracture).

Austen approaches history in the landscape from a different direction. In *Persuasion* the archeology of the landscape can almost be described as a kind of natural history. Certainly passages refer to "many a generation" passing away "since the first partial fall of the cliff [near Lyme] prepared the ground" for plowing (117). Austen's history focuses on the physical world and the changes of the seasons. Scott, however, carefully documents history through his endnotes and references to eyewitnesses. He even documents the superstitions and legends of Scottish culture by placing them in an historical context. Scott surrounds Jeanie's meeting with Queen Caroline in a heavy historical context that is decidedly missing in Austen novels. Most of Anne Elliot's landscapes reveal an emotional archeology of her memories, her personal, unrecorded recollections; Jeanie's thoughts reveal her as a typical heroic example of Scottish culture. Reciprocity exists between Anne and the landscape; it gives her a clearer recognition of what life means. Jeanie represents a figure in the landscape. Scott finds no need to change Jeanie; in fact, for a natural healthy Scotswoman to become too aware of her landscape, rather than just harmonizing with it, would be considered distracting for her and even presumptuous.

Scott's female characters are a natural extension of the landscape and, in Jeanie's case, can be so close to it as to be unaware of its true significance. When Jeanie's sister, Effie, tries to look at the landscape critically and artistically, she finds she is dabbling with something that is out of her control and learns her limitations, unlike Anne Elliot, who is liberated by relating to landscape in this way.

Although she shows her heroines relating to landscape in freer ways than most male writers, Austen never gets as far as showing a woman doing well entirely without the help of a man. Mrs. Croft and Anne need their men to experience the stimulating naval life, and they need the men to share their experiences with. (Maybe this is one of Lady Russell's problems; she has not found a "good man.") The right man for Anne has to have her view of the landscape as well, and Frederick Wentworth does. It is interesting to note how he connects her character with the landscape of the novel.

> Her character was now fixed on his mind as perfection itself, maintaining the loveliest medium of fortitude and gentleness; but he was obliged to acknowledge that only at Uppercross had he learnt to do her justice, and only at Lyme had he begun to understand himself. (242)

Lyme gave him "lessons"; "the scenes at the Cobb ... fixed her superiority" (242). So, to Wentworth, Anne is a person in her own right and yet ever connected with the landscape and the memories of past landscapes.

Austen shows Anne Elliot connecting with a landscape where neither complete domination nor submission is required of her. What she does seek is to understand it, and through the landscape to understand herself. The biological survival opportunities of landscape, the emotional survival available in the landscape, and the literary and artistic merit of the scenery are all things Anne recognizes. Of course, Austen has not cut her heroine off from society altogether. She needs the connections of a good man and the understanding of society to some degree, but Anne pushes her boundaries outward as much as she dares. She never intends to stay on her "little elevation in the garden" to see her world.

Austen has more in mind for her heroine here than Hannah More's societally connected notion of staying in the garden at Kellynch. Anne Elliot does not see herself as competitive, "in the race for the prize" of a man. Austen is neither as conservative as More, nor as radical as someone like Mary Wollestonecraft, who openly criticized the male literary tradition as well as women's addition to sentimental novels. She is instead concerned about Anne and her individual psychological well-being. Anne's fortuitous self-knowledge in a new landscape attracts Wentworth. We readers know that Anne could never permanently leave her stagnant position without him. She is going to sea, even though it will take a man to get her there. And if she once yielded to persuasion "exerted on the side of safety, not of risk" (244), at the end of the novel, she is now willing, even eager to risk the "dread of a future war ... dim[ming] her sunshine" (252) or the "tax of quick alarm" (252) as a part of naval life, if only she can retain that expansive, "oceanic" relationship to her landscape.

The heroine of *Persuasion* has been attracted to the coast, the liminal seashore, the English Channel, and after the end of the novel, maybe beyond. In Austen's last, and unfinished, novel, the sea is everything.

Chapter 7

Sanditon: Half Topography, Half Romance

> In reconciling the artificial with the natural we are seeking to reconcile the symbolism of our emancipation from the tyranny of environment with the symbolism of that same environment.
>
> —Appleton, *The Experience of the Landscape* (173)

E. M. Forster, who described himself as "slightly imbecile about Jane Austen," expressed his disappointment in her last uncompleted novel. He characterized *Sanditon* as a book which "promises little vigour of character and incident" (154).[1] However, Forster did understand that this novel fragment began by positioning landscape as a major character:

> There is a queer taste in these eleven chapters which is not easily defined: a double-flavoured taste—half topography, half romance. Sanditon is not like Lyme or Highbury or Northanger Abbey or the other places that provide scenes or titles to past novels. It exists in itself and for itself. Character-drawing, incident, and wit are on the decline, but topography comes to the front, and is screwed much deeper than usual into the story. (154)

Forster continued by asserting that "Sanditon gives out an atmosphere, and also exists as a geographic and economic force" (155). Returning to Austen scholar Brian Southam in his discussion of landscape throughout Austen's works: "Ultimately, in Sanditon, the setting becomes an agent in the story, a considerable element in the meaning of the work" (*Literary Manuscripts* 38).

Questions concerning the landscape of *Sanditon* include some of the following: Is the place what we, the readers, think it is? Or—can a place be what we wish it to be? Does the notion of a seaside resort represent the improver's dream or does it become that "double-flavoured" thing—half-topography, half-romance, as Forster characterized it? Or maybe both? We can only partially answer these questions because we may only speculate on how the novel might have been completed.

Every landscape viewer carries along his or her own perspective; one person's disintegrating hovel is another's romantic little cottage. Austen's seascape "improver," Mr. Parker, tumbling out of his carriage to see the cozy, little cottage by the wood (that zone of safety described by Appleton) announces:

---

[1] Not everyone feels the way Forster did. Brian Southam wrote extensively about *Sanditon* in *Jane Austen's Literary Manuscripts* (Oxford UP, 1964) arguing that this fragment, not only in its treatment of place but also in its style and character development, was remarkable. He called it "the most vigorous of all Jane Austen's writing," declaring that "there is not the least sign of fatigue in its style, invention, or design" (102).

"It could not have happened, you know, at a better place,—good out of evil ... *There*, I fancy lies my cure"—pointing to the neat-looking end of a cottage, which was seen romantically situated among wood on a high eminence at some little distance—"Does not *that* promise to be the very place?" (*MW* 364)

It turns out not to be "the very place"—nor his cure. (Or maybe it does denote his "cure," in that Mrs. Heywood ministers to his injury.) It seems to be the perfect aesthetic refuge, a place to hide and a place from which to seek, but Mr. Parker's assumptions are still wrong. What he assumes to be the surgeon's cottage is a much humbler tenement of a shepherd—"in spite of its spruce air at this distance" (366). Places are not what they seem.

The image of "the cottage" and its imaginary (or real) inhabitant comes up again a few pages later as Mr. Parker disparages Brinshore, the potential "competition" for Sanditon. When his new acquaintance, Mr. Heywood, claims never to have heard of Brinshore, Mr. Parker replies that "we may apply to Brinshore, that line of the poet Cowper in his description of the religious cottager, as opposed to Voltaire—'*She*, never heard of half a mile from home'" (370). It may be that Parker is connecting Brinshore and the cottager to illustrate the insignificance of both.

Many of Jane Austen's contemporaries would have been familiar with "Truth," the poem by William Cowper. Cowper was Jane Austen's "favourite moral writer" in verse, according to her brother Henry in *Biographical Notice of the Author*, prefixed to *Northanger Abbey* and *Persuasion* in 1818, and her contemporary readers would have undoubtedly seen the satirical intent in the twisting of these lines. Mr. Parker may want Sanditon to have "the mere tinsel" of a Voltaire rather than the "rich reward" of faith in obscure poverty. Some slippage, the twisting of meaning, exists in comparing Sanditon/Voltaire with Brinshore/the cottager. Where is "Truth" here?

Cowper begins his poem "Truth" with lines that cause the reader to understand how difficult it is to recognize reality in the landscape.

> Man on the dubious waves of error toss'ed,
> His ship half founder'd, and his compass lost,
> Sees far as human optics may command,
> A sleeping fog, and fancies it dry land:
> Spread all his canvass, ev'ry sinew plies,
> Pants for't, aims at it, enters it, and dies.
> Then farewell all self-satisfying schemes,
> His well-built systems, philosophic dreams,
> Deceitful views of future bliss, farewell! (1-9)

Perhaps Jane Austen was thinking of these lines too in connection with Mr. Parker. He might honestly be seeing "sleeping fog" and fancying it "dry land." Because he is misguided, he may be destroyed by his "self-satisfying schemes" and "well-built system" in attempting to transform Sanditon into a seaside resort.

Or Mr. Parker may simply be another, trying to win the race, that familiar analogy of evangelical writers. (See Hannah More's use of it in the *Persuasion* chapter.) A few lines later in "Truth," Cowper warns:

> He that would win the race must guide his horse
> Obedient to the customs of the course,
> Else, though unequall'd to the goal he flies,
> A meaner than himself shall gain the prize. (13-16)

Mr. Parker himself might envision what he is doing as "obedient to the customs of the course," in other words, helping the invalids of England find a true place of recovery by the sea—the real, true, good landscape. As we read this fragment of a novel, we can interpret Mr. Parker's schemes as "self-satisfying" and silly or just maybe more than that—"obedient to the customs of the course." After all, Mr. Parker, although he has some impractical schemes, is a likeable character, trying to improve the landscape (and seascape) for society's use. This use of poetry to wrench unintended meaning from it shows up again later in the story. In both situations, Austen is laughing at the misuse of poetical descriptions, even though the scene itself might really resemble the backwater little hamlet Parker thought it was.

The landscape that we are meant to see here seems to be half topography and half romance, partly accurate and partly imaginative. Topography *is* screwed much deeper than usual in this story. First, we have the romantic little cottage by the wood, yet one that is not really romantic. The cottage has been divided up and serves as a squalid dwelling for three poor old women and a shepherd. Still the cottage appears to be romantic, while serving a worthwhile purpose. (Maybe Mr. Parker, and by extension, Jane Austen, was thinking of one of the Gainsborough cottage scenes.) The next reference to a cottager is an imaginative one to disparage a real village, Brinshore, one probably containing cottages much like the earlier one that Parker had found so romantic. It is all about place and accuracy of representation and perspective. Landscape architect and Jane Austen admirer, Robert Benson, writes concerning the doubleness of *Sanditon*:

> Nature may have been reshaped and replaced by landscape in contemporary eyes, but Austen's vision evokes the idea of design *with* nature, the integration of art and artlessness, in both a literal and literary sense. This idea, and its expression in *Sanditon*, is like nothing else in her work. ("Jane Goes to Sanditon" 218)

The artless cottage and the artful cottage can be contained in the same structure. How can the real and imaginative Sanditon coexist? Mr. Parker, enthusiast and improver exclaims:

> Nature had marked it out—had spoken in most intelligent characters—The finest, purest sea breeze on the coast—acknowledged to be so—excellent bathing—fine hard sand—deep water ten yards from the shore—no mud—no weeds—no slimey rocks—Never was there a place more palpably designed by nature for the resort of the invalid. (369)

We need to remember that landscape (and seascape, to a certain extent) is not natural. Geographers frequently discuss the culturally constructed landscape and the artifice of it. Certainly, southern England, more than many places in the world, consists of layers of landscapes, with little that has not been changed by human hands. In *Across the Open Field*, Laurie Olin describes the landscape of southern England as a kind of narrative and the landscape architects as authors. (Capability

Brown says something very similar in the eighteenth century.) "Landscape architects and designers work in what might be described as a gap in the differences between the way things are and what might be, a gap that also holds out great potential," writes Olin (8-9). I believe that Austen (and Parker) is working with that gap in mind. Austen can poke fun at Parker's overblown enthusiasm, but, in *Sanditon*, she is attempting to bridge that gap herself—the gap between what is and what might be, between topography and romance.[2]

This "gap" is very much like the narratological one Genette mentions when he describes what lies between the metaphor and the thing for which it stands. Parker's Sanditon equates to health and well-being for the people who travel there. The gap is the interaction between the real and the imaginary topography. Parker's imaginary scene is the resort sales pitch:

> Nobody could catch cold by the sea, nobody wanted appetite by the sea, nobody wanted spirits, nobody wanted strength. They were healing, softening, relaxing—fortifying and bracing—seemingly just as was wanted—sometimes one, sometimes the other. –If the sea breeze failed, the seabath was the certain corrective;—and where bathing disagreed, the sea breeze alone was evidently designed by nature for the cure. (373)

But the sales hyperbole fills in the gap only if Parker believes it and can get others to believe it as well, although part of that same metaphorical gap is filled by a Sanditon which is, in reality, a topographical twin of Brinshore.

Part of this "gap" represents for Austen a dilemma of aesthetic geography: Where is the safest, happiest, best place to be in the landscape? The old, practical notion of house placement in a little valley a couple of miles from the sea clashes with the more romantic notion of the sublime view. When Charlotte Haywood points to "a very snug-looking place" (169) on the way to Sanditon, Parker tells her it is his old house:

> Our ancestors always built in a hole,—Here were we, pent down in this little contracted nook, without air or view, only one mile and three quarters from the noblest expanse of ocean between the south foreland and the land's end, and without the smallest advantage from it. You will not think I have made a bad exchange, when we reach Trafalgar House. (380)

As was mentioned earlier here, less than a decade after Austen wrote *Sanditon*, *The Tourist's Grammar; or Rules Relating to the Scenery and Antiquities Incident To Travellers* by Rev. T. D. Fosbroke was published (London: John Nichols and Son, 1826). In this *Grammar*, Fosbroke describes the way the landscape "ought be viewed," according to Gilpin, Repton and other landscape viewers and improvers of the first quarter of the nineteenth century. If Mr. Parker had had access to *Grammar*, he might have been able to spout out some bald statements such as, "Hills seen from

---

[2] Phillipa Tristram, in "Jane Austen and the Changing Face of England" from *The Georgian Country House: Architecture, Landscape and Society* (Frome, England: Sutton, 1998, pp. 139-151), observes that the changing face of England is most evident in *Sanditon*. "On the balance, [Austen] seems to have welcomed the 'state of alteration' which had overtaken the society of country villages, but whether it did, or did not, amount to an 'improvement' was a matter for each specific case" (151).

a low point may be less grand" or "Extensive views cannot be pleasing if bounded by a hard edge" (lxxxiv). Some of Fosbroke's statements are very similar to the prospects Jane Austen satirizes in *Sanditon*. For instance:

> The bay ... may be as picturesque as the lake; only the character of each is different ... Torbay is a fine specimen. Its form is semi-lunar. Its winding shores, on both sides, are screened with grand ramparts of rock, between which, in the central part, the ground from the country, forming a gentle vale, falls easily to the water's edge. (lxxxv)

It is not the scene that Jane Austen satirizes but the formulaic ways that landscape viewers and improvers insist are the only "approved" ways we have of viewing the scenes.

In a way, Parker might be called a small-time Humphry Repton, Repton with his plans for the Pavilion at Brighton, Parker with Trafalgar House at Sanditon.[3] Both are enthusiasts and improvers, looking for a more spectacular site for the house, both hide such unsightly views as kitchen gardens, and both envision the future with new plantations of trees and shrubbery which will mature in a generation. Repton apparently did not advise "siting a house directly over the sea" (Goode 44). Somehow Parker also manages to rationalize the new location as a safer place in a storm. When his wife comments that occupants of the valley hadn't felt the storms as the Parkers did in their exposed location, Parker explains that "'*We* have all the grandeur of the storm with less real danger, because the wind meeting with nothing to oppose or confine it around our house, simply rages and passes on'" (381).

In the description of the older house in the snug little valley, we as readers see safety and value and happiness, as well as Austen's satire on the practicality of landscape in fashion. But still, in this gap between the sublime prospect and safe location, Austen finds room to consider the future, the value in the imagined seaside, a constructed landscape, a palimpsest—new built atop the old. Trafalgar house "on the most elevated spot on the down" is "a light, elegant building" (384), and Charlotte, the potential heroine of this fragment, "found amusement enough in standing at her ample Venetian window, and looking over the miscellaneous foreground of unfinished buildings, waving linen, and tops of houses, to the sea, dancing and sparkling in sunshine and freshness" (384). She is an appreciative observer of the landscape here, one with room enough for laundry and an exhilarating view of the water. Views are so important to landscape improvers, such as Humphry Repton (and Mr. Parker) that the tolerance, and even pleasure, which Austen's purported heroine shows for this scene seems generous—an ability to the see the beauty of a prospect, even with its flaws. Austen has yet to develop much reader warmth for Charlotte; she seems like a less naïve version of Catherine Morland, one who recognizes the value of a seaside resort, and yet a female character who has enough maturity and knowledge to laugh at the gentleman prospect-maker. The new houses on "our health-breathing hill," as Mr. Parker calls it (383), are "looked at by Charlotte with the calmness of amused curiosity" (384).

---

[3] In fact, Roger Sales goes one step farther, comparing Parker to the Prince Regent in *Jane Austen and Representations of Regency England* (NY: Routledge, 1994) as Parker abandons his old house for a pavilion. He writes, "*Sanditon* may differ from these earlier writings by allowing obsession to become its main obsession" (213).

Sanditon's equation with health can encompass linen on the line and incomplete construction sites and still be exciting and healthful, yet amusing. In the gap there is also room for satirizing the overblown and stereotypical use of poetic description by such characters as Sir Edward—that poetry (he cannot quite remember which lines of Scott, but they influenced him greatly) "descriptive of the *indescribable* emotions they excite in the mind of sensibility" (396). Again, as with Mr. Parker's misuse of Cowper's lines, Sir Edward gets confused in his jumbled recollection of Scott. When Charlotte comments on the charming day and the southerly wind, Sir Edward replies, "Happy, happy wind, to engage Miss Heywood's thoughts!" and we, along with Charlotte, find him "downright silly" (398).

Ironically, Mr. Parker's brother and two sisters seem immune to the salubrious climate of Sanditon. It is a beautiful summer day, and yet they choose to sit as far away from the panoramic view of the sea as possible. The Parkers are described as a "family of imagination" (412), yet the brother and sisters mainly imagine ailments as actively and vividly as Mr. Parker imagines the curative properties of the seascape at Sanditon. Not only do they turn away from the view from their window, but also they avoid any energetic walks along the water, claiming the air to be too damp. Arthur Parker claims "a damp air does not like me" (415). The gap between the real and imaginative, the literal and literary, art and artlessness consists of half topography, half romance. The same landscape which looks toward a "dancing and sparkling" sea has room for pseudo-literary sensibility and hypochondria, all the while focusing on topography "screwed deeply into the story."

Where Charlotte finds the necessary personal history to view the seaside resort of Sanditon both with admiration and humor is unclear. She is young, the daughter of a gentleman farmer, and has traveled little. Yet, her unsentimental, clear thinking allows her to see both the "putrifying seaweed" and the "sea, dancing and sparkling in sunshine and freshness" and reconcile the new artificial "improvements" of a resort with the previously older and "unimproved" natural environment.

As in *Persuasion*, the heroine learns how to act from the landscape as well, but this time she eavesdrops on a scene which does not affect her personally as much as Anne is affected, overhearing from her position in the hedgerow, Louisa Musgrove and Captain Wentworth discussing her. The scene I am about to describe is the last one we have in this, the last fragmentary fictional piece of Jane Austen. This scene is a liminal one, existing on the boundary, literally right outside the park palings of Sanditon House, but also liminal in terms of being on the threshold of impropriety with the tête à tête of Clara Brereton and Edward Denham. An aesthetic geographer might look at this scene as the ideal place to hide and seek, yet it only *seems* to be private—Charlotte discovers the couple unbeknownst to them.

The topography of this scene begins on "a close, misty morning" on "the brow of the hill" (425), a scene deliberately obscured, only to be viewed with difficulty through a "vacant space" in the trees. Then we have the last perspective on the entrance to the estate ever written by Jane Austen:

> The road to Sanditon House was a broad, handsome, planted approach, between fields, and conducting at the end of a quarter of a mile through second gates into the grounds, which though not extensive had all the beauty and respectability which an abundance of very fine timber could give.—These entrance gates were so much in a corner of the

grounds or paddock, so near one of its boundaries, that an outside fence was at first almost pressing on the road—till an angle *here*, and a curve *there* threw them to a better distance. The fence was a proper park paling in excellent condition; with clusters of fine elms, or rows of old thorns following its line almost everywhere. (426)

The approach to the estate is very important to the narration of any story, both for Austen and Repton as both in their own way try to "improve" the scene. Repton seems frequently to be "troubled" by approaches as he describes one in his Redbook on Hatchlands in Surrey: "The approach ... is at present very objectionable, because after passing within view of the east front of the house, it runs round on the outside of the park pale." He criticizes the approach as coming too near the road and suggests "new plantations by the road side" will "conceal the house from almost every part of the road." In the Sanditon House scene, Austen shows her awareness of how a landscape improver might appraise the approach to the estate: Sanditon House is no Pemberley, but it has much to recommend it. The flaw in the design of the approach is lack of privacy for the estate.

Alistair Duckworth, in *The Improvement of the Estate*, suggests that this scene is "asymmetrical and disjointed ... a symbolic representation of a once worthy society twisted into a troubling new shape" (229). To my mind, the grounds are reminiscent of Sotherton in *Mansfield Park*—an old estate, venerable and heavily wooded, "proper," "respectable." Like the grounds of Sotherton, a hidden spot for private conversation has been found. But just as the spot is a place to hide, it is also a place to seek, and Charlotte, due to keen powers of observation, detects the couple's seemingly safe haven. Austen describes the scene this way:

> Charlotte could not but think of the extreme difficulty which secret lovers must have in finding a proper spot for their stolen interviews—Here perhaps they had thought themselves so perfectly secure from observation!—the whole field open before them—a steep bank and pales never crossed by the foot of man at their back—and a great thickness of air, in aid—. Yet here, she had seen them. They were really ill-used. (427)

Emma had knowledge of Jane Fairfax wandering in a field when she claimed to be ill. Anne Elliot had knowledge of what was going on in Captain Wentworth's mind from her position in the hedgerow. Now another female protagonist transgresses (unknowingly) on the scene and knows more about the narrative than she did before, transforming the scene. Charlotte's height and alertness allow her a prospect beyond any More may have imagined from the "little elevation" in the garden. Charlotte enjoys a fair degree of safety, as well as freedom to see without being seen. The lovers are not "safe." A female gaze penetrates this artificial landscape, with its park palings and plantings. Charlotte sees something she describes as "white and womanish" on the other side of the park paling (427). These almost ethereal adjectives add an air of mystery to the scene she sees; in a sense hers is a feminine gaze, yet it objectifies another woman. Still it is a gaze that feels abashed at what is seen—"they were really ill-used," and she sympathizes with them. That Charlotte does not condemn the couple may be the beginning of the reader's sympathy for her.

Cresswell emphasizes that place is more than just geography, that it "intersects with sociocultural expectations" (8). He observes that looking at space when things appear to be going wrong can help us question the so-called "naturalness" of geography. (We have already seen that landscape improvers, such as Repton, bend the "naturalness" of the landscape to suit a certain culturally based pleasure in the scene.) Cresswell uses the word "transgression" to discuss how place is used to question the naturalness of the world. He claims that "uses and limits of transgression [can act] as a way of challenging and transforming ... beliefs" (150). Women have transgressed and transformed geography before in Jane Austen's work, leaving their mark: witness Elizabeth Bennet at Pemberley, Emma at Box Hill, and presumably Anne Eliott as she goes to sea.

At Sanditon, Charlotte Heywood may be one more woman changing the way space is seen. In the last scene from this fragmentary novel, the naturalness of setting is questioned. Charlotte transgresses in a way that may have a chance of changing the way a place is viewed, yet she herself may be only gradually aware of that ability. She may be the "private commentator" Duckworth describes her as, but she is not quite the "neutral observer" (218), and probably if this story were to continue, Charlotte would find it increasingly difficult to remain neutral as well. This scene intrigues us as readers, what with the "white ribbons" seen through a "vacant space" in spite of "a great thickness of air" by "observant eyes" (427). The characters seem to be so tied to a landscape here that the narrator promises much more. The key to our understanding the meaning of a place like Sanditon, the watering place, and Sanditon House, the old estate, as well as Willingden and Brinshore, the geography of the southeast coast of England, may lie with Charlotte. She has the ability to "transgress" and possibly "transform" the landscape as she observes more and forms new judgments, questioning the naturalness of the old, low-lying places and the new "sparkling views" of the sea.

Most critics agree that this last extended piece of writing by Austen seems to be going in new directions. Robert Benson writes, "In creating *Sanditon*, Jane Austen looks ahead and designs, even as a landscape gardener might, a scene in which nature and technology merge in the futuristic, as well as in the physical sense" (216). I agree and also notice that Austen's work here seems to look forward to the nascent improvers' seaside resorts and the places that the Prince Regent has already begun to cultivate. And yet her satire in this last work stands out more than it does in *Persuasion*. Southam sees characters such as Diana Parker, Arthur, and Sir Edward as part of "a small gallery of human absurdity" (110). Although I certainly believe Austen is making an attempt to try new things, she also seems to retrieve some of the sharper satirical scenes of her youth. Landscape is "screwed in" tightly to those scenes as well, as we remember Mr. Gower at Evelyn and Sophia running mad in the landscape of "Love and Freindship."

Having completed examining this fragment, we are still not sure what Sanditon will turn out to be, but we do know that Austen is using both satire and romance to describe the seaside resort and its environs. A house on a hill overlooking the ocean is both impractical due to heavy weather and exciting for the same reason. Her prospective heroine, Charlotte Heywood, sees the landscape with both a satirical eye and an eye toward mystery and romance. In each case, the landscape of Sanditon stands out as much as any of the characters do, and the feminine gaze upon the landscape and seascape might prove true Forster's notion of *Sanditon* as a "double-flavoured thing—half-topography, half romance."

Chapter 8

Some Nineteenth-Century Reactions, Twenty-First Century Women in the Landscape and Final Remarks

"Why do you like Miss Austen? I am puzzled on that point?" Charlotte Brontë asks George Lewes in a letter more than twenty years after Jane Austen's death (*The Brontës* 179-80). One of Brontë's main complaints about *Pride and Prejudice* involves landscape. Brontë claims that Austen adhered to the "cultivated garden, with neat borders and delicate flowers." She goes on to mention the "confined houses," which she finds irritating as well.

Earlier responses to Austen were generally more favorable, although reviews were few; in fact, *Mansfield Park* was neglected entirely. One of the earliest articles in *The Critical Review* (February 1812) examines *Sense and Sensibility* shortly after it was published. The reviewer begins by criticizing the "multiplicity" of novels being published at the time but admits that *Sense and Sensibility* by "a Lady" can "claim this fair praise" because it contains a "useful lesson" and the "incidents are probable, and highly pleasing, and interesting" (149). The author singles out one of Austen's satirical scenes on landscape where Marianne becomes annoyed with Edward Ferrars' practical reaction to what she deems to be "the picturesque." The reviewer, obviously entertained by the scene, comments, "In the jargon of landscape scenery, Elinor's lover was a mere *ignoramus*; he gave things, objects, and persons, their proper names, a crime which could not be overlooked" (152), and certainly not by one with the overblown sensibility of Marianne. So this "most excellent lesson to young ladies to curb that violent sensibility" (152) gains approval for Austen's first published novel.

Pride and Prejudice, reviewed the following year in *The British Critic*, received even higher praise than its predecessor:

> It is very far superior to almost all the publications of the kind which have lately come before us. It has a very unexceptionable tendency, the story is well told, the characters remarkably well drawn and supported, and written with great spirit as well as vigour. (189)

The novel was also reviewed the same year in *The Critical Review*; however, this review focuses mostly on Mr. and Mrs. Bennet, generally the most "confined" characters and, again, reiterates the importance of the "lesson" learned—this time from Lydia's elopement; however, the landscape is altogether ignored. Walter Scott was the first major figure to express admiration for Austen's work. In an unsigned review for *Quarterly Review*, he wrote that *Emma* "reminds us something of the merits of the Flemish school of painting. The subjects are not often elegant, and certainly never grand; but they are finished up to nature, and with a precision which delights the reader" (197). Noting this major artistic landscape painting tradition reinforces the importance of the outdoors in Austen's novels.

Finally, shortly after Austen's death and the publication of *Northanger Abbey* and *Persuasion* together, a writer for the *British Critic* noted that Austen "seems to have no other object in view, than simply to paint some of those scenes which she has herself seen, and which every one, indeed, may witness daily" (297). Certainly readers of her letters know that this authenticity of setting is what Austen valued most. Again this reviewer connects painting and literature in Austen's work, concentrating almost entirely on *Northanger Abbey*:

> [F]or if the people and the scenes which she has chosen, as the subjects of her composition be not painted with perfect truth, with exact and striking resemblance, the whole effect ceases; her characters have no kind of merit in themselves, and whatever interest they excite in the mind of the reader, results almost entirely, from the unaccountable pleasure, which, by a peculiarity in our nature, we derive from a simple imitation of any object, without any reference to the abstract value or importance of the object itself. This fact is notorious in painting; and the novels of Miss Austen alone, would be sufficient to prove, were proof required, that the same is true in the department of literature, which she adored. (298)

Thus this early reviewer seemed to understand what Jane Austen was about: the painted and novelistic scenes must remain true to what actually exists, with no attempt to impose some abstract, constructed value upon them. Unfortunately the entire review focuses upon *Northanger Abbey*, dismissing *Persuasion* as "a much less fortunate performance than that which we have just been considering" (302). The reviewer notes that Austen's last novel is inferior to *Northanger Abbey*, mainly become of "its moral, which seems to be, that young people should always marry according to their own inclinations" (302), a moral of which he obviously disapproves.

By writing a generally restrained description of the landscape, Austen gives the reader a chance to fill in the gap between what she does describe and what is in the reader's imagination. Just as Jane Austen instantly knew Jane Bingley when she saw her in a particular portrait at a London gallery, she was also intimately acquainted with her landscape. (As Chesterton wrote, "She knew what she knew ... she did not know what she did not know" (*Critics* 20). She would not write about people or landscapes without really knowing either, so she would not write a romance about the "House of Saxe Cobourg" (*Letters* 312) even at the suggestion of the Prince Regent's librarian. Her deliberately spare landscape descriptions made sense to her; she expected her readers imaginatively to fill in the gaps. And yet she sought verisimilitude, wanting to know whether there were hedgerows in Northampton so that the characters might react properly in that landscape. The landscape descriptions and interaction with the heroines become doubly important for the reader to notice and interpret. Ways of interpreting how the heroines interact in their landscapes open up more and more with new readings of Austen.

In Brontë's critique of the "carefully fenced, highly cultivated garden, with neat borders and delicate flowers," Brontë ignored the landscapes which meant so much to Austen's heroines—the high downs of Devonshire where Marianne met

Willoughby, the magnificence of Pemberley, Box Hill, and the seacoast of Lyme Regis. As we examine Austen's landscapes more closely, we find that flowers, and even carefully cultivated gardens, are scarcely ever mentioned, with the exception of Mr. Collins's garden, and, of course, the reader understands the satirical tone concerning all matters involving Mr. Collins. When Brontë mentions the "confined houses," she does not seem to recognize that most of the major events in the stories of Austen's heroines occur outdoors. In fact, Austen's landscapes that gave the heroines the energy and confidence to find personal freedom were not so different from those of Brontë herself—in some ways landscapes that become part of the heroine.

Although Charlotte Brontë had no great admiration for Jane Austen's novels, both Brontë and Austen situate their heroines similarly as active participants in the landscape where women recognize their own ambivalence over landscape control and the potential danger of a male presence trying to objectify them. For instance, Lucy Snowe, heroine of Brontë's *Villette*, uses her position to construct a landscape in her mind, a feminine zone of compromise between prospect and refuge. This spot remains one of the richest examples of edge-of-the-wood landscape:

> Conceive a dell, deep-hollowed in forest secrecy; it lies in dimness and mist: its turf is dank, its herbage pale and humid. A storm or an axe makes a wide gap amongst the oak-trees; the breeze sweeps in; the sun looks down; the sad cold dell becomes a deep cup of luster; high summer pours her blue glory and her golden light out of that beauteous sky, which till now the starved hollow never saw. (*Villette* 216)

In the dell, hope, as well as danger, exists, and, instead of being an insignificant figure, as Lucy saw herself in a shipwreck picture earlier in the novel, Lucy's mind *is* the dell itself. In this scene, nature is managed. Clear-cutting occurs presumably for the good of the landscape, and the real and ideal become tentatively reconciled. Hope certainly begins to reveal itself when the "sad cold dell" becomes a "deep cup of luster, even as a result of what seems an unfeeling, unnatural clear-cutting. Lucy finds a way to stay within nature and yet stay outside of it at the same time. She has been able to encompass a landscape within her mind, something that never quite happens with Austen's heroines. Given the proper economic and psychological conditions, Lucy Snowe's response to her surroundings eventually makes the physical presence of a man unnecessary.

Austen's landscapes for heroines do have some similarities to Brontë's, although the completely imaginary landscape in the mind of the heroine Austen never shows. Austen was a realist; an essential cultural element to which all the heroines in her six novels acquiesce is marriage. At the end of each novel, the heroine finds a way of controlling her landscape chiefly by attracting a mate who understands her and her place in the landscape. Austen could not completely discard this plot convention; marriage is still required. (But we do not know for certain whether *Sanditon* would have ended with marriage or not.) The marriages always further the heroines' sense of autonomy in the landscape. With her last novel, *Persuasion*, we see Anne Elliot, pushed out of her home, and, just as Lucy, she finds herself homeless. Yet, Anne finds a new home, at the brink of transgressing what had previously been the boundaries of strictly male territory—the sea. Here she encounters the distinct possibility of transforming her life and the potential available to a woman who moves beyond simply viewing her world from a "little elevation in her garden," as Hannah More suggested—and really as Brontë *believes* that Austen suggested as well. Had Austen lived long enough, one of her female characters might have done what Brontë's did—found a way to lead a life without marriage as the happy ending.

***

In the late twentieth century and beyond, traveling women do write about their solitary experiences in the landscape and how they are affected by them. Some of the arguments I have made about Austen's use of landscapes follow through and push beyond what Austen has done to suggest a special emotional connection with the landscape for her heroines and its use to develop their inner lives. Alison Russell, in the Coda, "Whither the Women?" from *Crossing Boundaries: Postmodern Travel Literature*, writes, "The gendering of travel and travel writing ... is ... indicated by women's awareness of their own physicality—their female bodies and physical experience of place and space" (191-192). Mary Morris, novelist and travel writer, asserts that "'because of the way that women have cultivated their inner lives, a journey often becomes a dialogue between the inner and outer, between our emotional necessity and the reality of the external world'" (qtd. in Russell 191).

Russell suggests that because of "the distinctions between men and women's travel writing, women's travel literature might best be studied as a 'genre of its own'" (193). Using Gillian Rose's *Feminism and Geography* to support her claim, Russell mentions many of the same obstacles that Austen's heroines encountered in the landscape: vulnerability in negotiating a space where the women sense they are watched, patriarchal ownership, difficulty negotiating socially constructed boundaries of gender and "exclusion from, or confinement within, spaces that have been mapped, controlled, and designed by men" (194).

Russell discusses five texts by women travel writers in this chapter, and she suggests that what they have in common are a "felt experience of public and personal spaces, both past and present, ... a common interest in reconfiguring, or defamiliarizing, masculinist perspectives of travel, travel writing, and geography" (204). Following an abusive childhood, Jenny Diski, in *Skating to Antarctica: A Journey to the End of the World*, searches for a "place of safety, a white oblivion" (2). Russell comments that Diski's "desire for the blankness of Antarctica" (215) seems to coincide with women's difficulty in dealing with landscape and their attempt to become invisible there. As we have found with some of Austen's heroines, Diski finds herself in a "position of being prisoner and exile, both within and without" (Rose 189). Other texts, such as Julia Blackburn's *The Emperor's Last Island: A Journey to St. Helena* and Sheila Nickerson's *Disappearance: A Map*, deal with the lives of exiles or lost people in remote areas. Blackburn uses landscape as "a means of locating absence," according to Russell (201), as Nickerson deals with her place in many locations at once—"there and not—there" (Russell 199). Nickerson expresses her ambivalence in mapping space: "Any written statement is as true as the awareness and the intention of the writer at that moment, and awareness is always shifting" (108), and yet she constantly struggles to locate herself on the map. Even in the early twentieth-first century, women remain sensitive to their lack of mastery over the landscape, a control that many of their male counterparts have taken for granted. Both Blackburn and Nickerson have a fear of "disappearing," a fear that has made its way from Burney to Atwood and down to these twenty-first century women travel writers.

***

As was mentioned in Chapter 1, we cannot examine the function of landscape in Jane Austen's novels without consulting Alistair Duckworth's *The Improvement of the Estate*. In it Duckworth writes, "The estate as an ordered physical structure is a metonym for other inherited structures—society as a whole, a code of morality, a body of manners, a system of language—and 'improvements'" (xxix). Furthermore, he asserts that Austen's "mature novels [are] an authentic commitment to a social morality and a continuous awareness and exposure of attitudes destructive of social continuity" (xxxix). Certainly Austen felt that Pemberley, Mansfield Park, and Donwell Abbey stood for those values of philosopher-statesman Edmund Burke— that "'to improve' was to treat the deficient or corrupt parts of an established order ... [, not] to destroy all that had been built up by the 'collected reason of the ages'" (46-47). Austen concurred with Burke's idea of improvement, but, as we have seen in this study, Austen positions herself, as a woman novelist, in such a way as to agree with the improvers while allowing her heroines opportunities to search for what they most desire: freedom. The heroines had to find their freedom where they could, and usually that freedom (and sometimes safety and knowledge) was found on the boundaries or outside the grounds of the estates that were already pronounced by their male owners (and their landscape architect, Humphry Repton) as "best," "good," "bad," and "worst." Like Austen, her heroines must find their own "good" (or "not bad," as Repton would call them) prospects and refuges, even though they remain within the "established order."

Austen's female protagonists find this refuge in the environment while viewing the whole scene at a distance, and from this distance, gaining new insights. Her heroines learn much by staying in such a position as suggested by Palmer's "View from Rook's Hill"—a good place to hide and yet a good place to seek. The heroines from fiction as early as "Catharine,—Or The Bower" through the fragment, *Sanditon*, bring with them their own ways of seeing the landscape and succeeding in it.

As we have explored Austen's use of landscape, we have seen how she treats landscape differently than do her contemporary women writers. Austen takes an environment with which she is personally familiar and allows her heroines to identify with it, work with it, and find new confidence. Her heroines are no mere figures of national pride to be gazed upon as objects; they resist being regarded as part of the natural scenery and they certainly prevail in landscapes that are many times perilous. Austen's heroines progress from young women who find a refuge in a bower or an estate to Anne Elliot of her final completed novel, *Persuasion*, who loses a home, only to look outward, beyond the range of Austen's previous heroines, to the potential of a far less confining and far more satisfying place to live. In Austen's last work (which she called "The Brothers") everything is in flux. The setting begins to take on a prominence not seen since her early years. We will never know how Austen's future landscapes might have assisted her heroines in finding fulfillment. Both when Charlotte Heywood stood at the edge of a cliff as it precipitously dropped to the sea and while she stood in the woods at the edge of the estate's park palings, we realize that Austen's heroines will continue to find for themselves a good place to hide and a good place to seek.

Bibliography

Addison, Joseph. *The Spectator.* 465, 12 August 1712.
Alexander, Christine. "The Prospect of Blaise: Landscape and Perception in *Northanger Abbey.*" *Persuasions* 21(1999): 17-31.
Altomari, Lisa. "Jane Austen and her Outdoors." *Persuasions* 12 (1990): 51-53.
Andrews, Malcolm. *The Search for the Picturesque: Landscape, Aesthetics, and Tourism in Britain, 1760-1800.* Stanford: Stanford UP, 1989.
Appleton, Jay. *The Experience of the Landscape.* New York: John Wiley and Sons, 1975.
"Article 17." *British Critic* 41 (February 1813): 189-190.
"Article V." *British Critic* N.59 (1818): 293-301.
"Article V." *The Critical Review* 4th Series 3 (February 1812): 149-152.
"Article X." *The Critical Review* 4th Series 3 (March 1813): 318-324.
Atwood, Margaret. *Wilderness Tips.* NY: Bantam, 1991.
Austen, Henry. "Biographical Note." *The Works of Jane Austen.* Ed. R. W. Chapman. 3rd. Ed. Oxford: OUP, 1933. 3-9.
Austen, Jane. *Jane Austen's Letters.* Ed. Deirdre LeFaye. 3rd ed. Oxford: OUP, 1995.
———, *The Works of Jane Austen.* Ed. R. W. Chapman. 3rd. Ed. Oxford: OUP, 1933.
Austen-Leigh, J. E. *A Memoir of Jane Austen.* London: MacMillan, 1906.
Bachelard, Gaston. *The Poetics of Space.* Trans. Maria Jolas. Boston: Beacon, 1969.
Bal, Mieke. *Narratology: The Introduction to the Theory of Narrative.* Trans. Christine VanBoheemen. Buffalo: U of Toronto P, 1985.
Balzac, Honoré. *La Rabouilleuse.* Paris: Garnier Brothers, 1996.
Barrell, John. *The Political Theory of Painting from Reynolds to Hazlitt.* New Haven: Yale UP, 1986.
Batey, Mavis. *Jane Austen and the English Landscape.* London: Barn Elms P, 1996.
———, *Regency Gardens.* Buckinghamshire: Shire Publications, 1995.
Benson, Robert. "Jane Goes to Sanditon: An Eighteenth Century Lady." *Persuasions* 19 (1997): 211-218.
Bermingham, Ann. *Landscape and Ideology: The English Rustic Tradition, 1740-1860.* Berkeley: U of CA P, 1986.
Brontë, Charlotte. *Villette.* NY: Houghton Mifflin, 1971.
Burke, Edmund. *The Correspondence of Edmund Burke.* Eds. Alfred Cobban and Robert Smith. 10 vols. Chicago: U of Chicago P, 1967.
———, *A Philosophical Enquiry into the Origin of Our Ideas of the Sublime and Beautiful.* Ed. James Boulton. Notre Dame: U of Notre Dame P, 1980.
Burney, Fanny. *Evelina.* NY: Norton, 1965.
Carter, George, Patrick Goode and Kedrun Laurie. *Humphry Repton: Landscape Gardener.* London: Sainsbury Centre for Visual Arts, 1982.

Collins, Irene. *Jane Austen: The Parson's Daughter*. London: Hambleton P, 1998.
Cooper, William. *Cooper: Verse and Letters Selected by Brian Spiller*. Cambridge: Harvard UP, 1968.
Cosgrove, Denis and Stephen Daniels. *Iconography of Landscape*: NY: Cambridge P, 1988.
Cosgrove, Denis. *Social Formations and Symbolic Landscape*. Totowa, NJ: Barnes and Noble, 1984.
Craik, Kenneth. "Psychological Reflections on Landscape." *Meanings and Values*. Eds. Edmund Penning-Rowsell and David Lowenthal. Boston: Allen and Unwin, 1986.
Cresswell, Tim. *In Place/Out of Place: Geography, Ideology, and Transgression*. U of Minneapolis P, 1996.
Critics on Jane Austen. Ed. Judith O'Neill. Coral Gables: U of Miami P, 1970.
Daniels, Stephen. *Humphry Repton: Landscape Gardening and the Geography of Georgian England*. New Haven: Yale UP, 1999.
Destinations: Cultural Landscapes of Tourism. Ed. Greg Ringer. NY: Routledge, 1999.
Doody, Margaret Anne. *Frances Burney: The Life in the Works*. New Brunswick, NJ, Rutgers UP, 1988.
———, "The Short Fiction." *The Cambridge Companion to Jane Austen*. Eds. Edward Copeland and Juliet McMaster. Cambridge: Cambridge UP, 1997. 84-99.
Duckworth, Alistair. *The Improvement of the Estate: A Study of Jane Austen's Novels*. Baltimore: JHU P, 1994.
———, "Nature." *The Jane Austen Companion*. Ed. J. David Grey. NY: MacMillan, 1986. 317-319.
Edwards, Anne-Marie. *In the Steps of Jane Austen*. Newbury, UK: Countryside Books, 1979.
Eisenman, Stephen. *Nineteenth-Century Art*. 2nd ed. London: Thames & Hudson, 2002.
Forster, E. M. *Abbinger Harvest*. Rahway, NJ: Quinn & Boden, 1936.
Fosbroke, Rev. T. D. *The Tourist's Grammar; or rules relating to the Scenery and Antiquities incident to Travellers; compiled from The first authorities and including an epitome of Gilpin's principles of the Picturesque*. London: John Nichols and Son, 1826.
Genette, Gerard. *Figures of Literary Discourse*. Trans. Jane E. Lewin. Ithaca: Cornell UP, 1980.
Gilbert, Sandra M. and Susan Gubar. *The Madwoman in the Attic: The Woman Writer and the Nineteenth-Century Literary Imagination*. New Haven: Yale UP, 1979.
Gilpin, William. *Three Essays: On Picturesque Beauty; On Picturesque Travel; and On Sketching Landscape*. London: Cadell and Davies, 1808.
Gordon, George. "Don Juan." *Byron*. Jerome J. McGann, ed. NY: Oxford UP, 1986. 426.
Herle, Jeffrey. "Introduction." *Catharine,—Or the Bower*. Ed. Juliet McMaster. Edmonton, Can.: Juvenila P, 1996.
Heydt-Stevenson, Jill. "Liberty, Connection and Tyranny: The Novels of Jane Austen and the Aesthetic Movement of the Picturesque." *Lessons of*

Romanticism: A Critical Companion. Eds. Thomas Pfau and Robert F. Gleckner. Durham: Duke UP, 1998.

Hipple, Walter J. *The Beautiful, the Sublime, and the Picturesque in Eighteenth-century British Aesthetic Theory*. Carbondale, Ill: Southern Ill UP, 1957.

Honan, Park. *Jane Austen*. NY: St. Martin's P, 1987.

Hughes, George. "The Semiological Realization of Space." *Cultural Landscapes of Tourism*. Ed. Greg Ringer. NY: Routledge, 1998.

Hunt, John Dixon. *Gardens and the Picturesque*. Cambridge: MIT P, 1992.

Jackson, J. B. "The Vernacular Landscape." *Landscape Meanings and Values*. Eds. Edmund Penning-Rowell and David Lowenthal. Boston: Allen and Unwin, 1986.

Johnson, Claudia. *Jane Austen: Women, Politics, and the Novel*. Chicago: U of Chicago P, 1988.

Kaplan, Deborah. *Jane Austen Among Women*. Baltimore: Johns Hopkins UP, 1992.

Kroeger, Karl. *Romantic Landscape Vision: Constable and Wordsworth*. Madison: U of Wisconsin P, 1975.

Levine, George. *Darwin and the Novelists*. Cambridge: Harvard, 1988.

———, *The Realistic Imagination*. Chicago: U of Chicago P, 1981.

Lorraine, Tamsin. *Gender, Identity, and the Production of Meaning*. Boulder: Westview P, 1990.

Luckàcs, Georg. *The Historical Novel*. Trans. Hannah and Stanley Mitchell. London: Merlin P, 1962.

McMaster, Julia. "The Short Fiction: Energy vs. Sympathy."

Malins, Edward. *English Landscape and Literature, 1660-1840*. NY: Oxford UP, 1966.

Meinig, D. W. *The Interpretation of Ordinary Landscapes: Geographical Essays*. NY: Oxford UP, 1979.

Moers, Ellen. *Literary Women*. Garden City, NY: Doubleday, 1976.

More, Hannah. *Coelebs, In Search of a Wife*. 3rd ed. 2 vols. London: T. Cadell and W. Davies, 1809, vol. 1.

———, *Strictures on the Modern System of Female Education*. 2 vols. NY: Garland, 1974.

Nokes, David. *Jane Austen: A Life*. Berkeley: U of CA P, 1997.

Olin, Laurie. *Across the Open Field: Essays from English Landscape*. Philadelphia, U of PA P, 2000.

Ortner, Sherry. "Is Female to Male as Nature Is to Culture?" *Woman, Culture, and Society*. Eds. Michelle Zimbalist Rosaldo and Louise Lamphere. Stanford: Stanford UP, 1974.

Proulx, Annie. "Big Skies, Empty Places." *The New Yorker*. 25 Dec. 2000, 1 Jan. 2001: 139.

Radcliffe, Ann. *The Mysteries of Udolpho*. London: Oxford UP, 1966.

Repton, Humphry. *The Red Book of Ferney Hall*. J. P. Morgan Library, NY.

———, *The Red Book of the Hatchlands*. J. P. Morgan Library, NY.

Ringer, Greg. "Introduction." *Cultural Landscapes of Tourism*. NY: Routledge, 1998.

Rose, Gillian. *Feminism and Geography: The Limits of Geographical Knowledge*. Minneapolis: U Minn P, 1993.

Ross, Marlon. "Naturalizing Gender: Woman's Place in Wordsworth's Ideological Landscape." *ELH* 53 (1986): 391-410.
Russell, Alison. *Crossing Boundaries: Postmodern Travel Literature*: NY: Palgrave, 2000.
Sales, Roger. *Closer to Home: Writers and Places in England, 1780-1830.* Cambridge: Howard, 1986.
Scott, Walter. "Introduction." *The Fortunes of Nigel*. By Walter Scott. Lincoln: U of Nebraska P, 1965.
———, *The Heart of Midlothian*. Oxford: Oxford UP, 1982.
———, An unsigned review of Emma. *Quarterly Review* 14 (1815): 188-201.
Snyder, W. C. "Mother Nature's Other Natures: Landscape in Women's Writing, 1770-1830." *Women's Studies.* 21 (1992): 143-162.
Sopher, David. "The Landscape of Home: Myth, Experience, Social Meaning." *The Interpretation of Ordinary Landscapes.* Ed. D. W. Meinig. NY: Oxford UP, 1979.
Southam, Brian. *Jane Austen's Literary Manuscripts*. London: OUP, 1964.
Spacks, Patricia. *The Female Imagination*. NY: Avon, 1975.
Sulloway, Alison. *Jane Austen and the Province of Womanhood*. Philadelphia: U of PA P, 1989.
Tanner, Tony. Introduction. *Mansfield Park*. NY: Penguin Books, 1965. 7-36.
———, Introduction. *Pride and Prejudice*. NY: Penguin Books, 1972. 7-46.
———, Introduction. *Sense and Sensibility*. NY: Penguin Books, 1969. 7-34.
Thacker, Christopher. *The History of Gardens*. London: Croom Helm, 1979.
Tristram, Philippa. "Jane Austen and the Changing Face of England." *The Georgian Country House: Architecture, Landscape, and Society*. Frome, England: Sutton, 1998.
Watkins, David. *The English Vision: The Picturesque in Architecture, Landscape, and Garden Design*. NY: Harper and Row, 1982.
Williams, Raymond. *Marxism and Literature.* NY: Oxford UP, 1977.
Wordsworth, William. *The Poetic Works of Wordsworth*. Paul D. Sheats, ed. Boston: Houghton Mifflin, 1982. 111.
———, *The Prelude 1799, 1805, 1850*. Eds. Jonathan Wordsworth et al. NY: Norton, 1979.

Index

(Jane Austen is JA throughout the index, except where she is the main entry. References to illustrations are in **bold**)

Altomari, Lisa 59
Andrews, Malcolm 27
 The Search for the Picturesque 6
Appleton, Jay x, xiii, 9, 11, 20–1, 23, 44, 50, 85, 87, 91, 92
 The Experience of Landscape 21
 zone of compromise, concept 16
Atwood, Margaret
 landscape in 2
 works
  'Death by Landscape' 2, 9, 13–15, 23
  Wilderness Tips 2
Austen, Jane
 cultural duality 4–5, 42
 geography, interest in 3, 68
 juvenilia 8
 liminality in 9, 59, 69–70, 98, 102, 108, 115
 and the picturesque 28
  writers on 6–8
 short fiction 31–2
 Sir Walter Scott, comparison 83–4, 99–102
 on Sweden 3
 works
  'Amelia Webster' 34
  'The Brothers' 115–16
  'Catharine – Or The Bower' 3, 38–40, 69, 87, 115
  Emma x, xi, xiii, 11, 63, 75–82, 83, 111–12
  'Evelyn' 35, 36, 37, 59, 64
  'Frederic and Elfrida' 32–3
  'Jack and Alice' 16, 33
  'Love and Freindship' 3, 34–5, 55
  Mansfield Park 11, 26, 63, 66–74, 87
  Northanger Abbey xii, 8, 10, 40, 43–50, 112
  Persuasion xii, 3, 11, 12, 38, 53, 74, 83–99, 101, 113, 115
  Pride and Prejudice 10, 40, 43, 56–60, 111
  Sanditon 8, 9, 11, 12, 16, 40, 85, 103–10
  Sense and Sensibility 8, 10, 40, 43, 52–6, 111
  The Watsons xii

Bachelard, Gaston 72
 The Poetics of Space 98
Bal, Mieke xiv
Barrell, John 66
Batey, Mavis, *Jane Austen and the English Landscape* 6
Bath
 JA on xii–xiii
 picturesque views 43
 setting for *Northanger Abbey* xii, 43–4, 45, 49
Beautiful, the, in *The Mysteries of Udolpho* 27
behaviour, and landscape 2
Benson, Robert 105, 110
Bermingham, Ann 76
Blackburn, Julia, *The Emperor's Last Island* 114
Blaise Castle 44, 49 n5
boundaries *see* liminality
Box Hill xiii–xiv, 61, 76, 78, 80–1, 82, 113
 in *Emma* xiii, xiv
 as zone of exposure 80
Bristol-Avon Canal xiii
British Critic 112
Brontë, Charlotte 12
 on JA 35, 111, 112–13
 liminality in 113
 Villette 113
Burke, Edmund 7, 68, 76, 79, 115
 Philosophical Enquiry 6, 26
Burney, Fanny 8, 9, 14

121

works
  Camilla 17
  Evelina 15, 16, 17–20, 29
Butler, Marilyn, *Jane Austen and the War of Ideas* 6–7

'Capability' Brown, Lancelot 25–6, 78
Chawton xi
Claude glass 2, 5, 6, 12, 24, 27, 44, 45, 72, 101
Claude Lorrain 2, 25
Cobb, Lyme Regis xi–xii, 42, 74, 96, 98
  as zone of exposure 91–2
Collins, Irene xii
Cosgrove, Denis
  on landscape 4, 5, 25, 41, 52, 65, 79, 100
  works
    Iconography of Landscape 5
    Landscape and Social Formation 65
    Social Formation and Symbolic Landscape 57
    The Idea of Landscape 5
'cottage' ix, 6, 34 n3, 48 n4, 58 n7, 72, 103–4, 105
Cowper, William, 'Truth' 104–5
Craik, Kenneth 99
Cresswell, Tim 2, 3–4, 75, 109–10
The Critical Review 111

Daniels, Stephen 5
Diski, Jenny, *Skating to Antarctica* 114
Donwell Abbey xi, 81–2, 115
Doody, Margaret Anne 17, 18, 32
  The Cambridge Companion to Jane Austen 31
Duckworth, Alistair 72
  The Improvement of the Estate 6, 7, 109, 115

edge-of-the-wood phenomenon, landscape 9, 21, 26, 29, 71, 91, 97, 101, 113
Edwards, Anne-Marie, *In the Steps of Jane Austen* xii
'elegance', in *Persuasion* 93
'enclaves of civility' 81
  Highbury as 78
  Mansfield Park as 67, 68, 74
  Stoneleigh Abbey as 78

feminism, and the picturesque 8, 27–8
flowers, in JA 47–8

Forster, E.M. 11
  on *Sanditon* 85, 103, 110
Fosbroke, T.D. *The Tourist's Grammar* 52, 106–7

Gainsborough, Thomas
  Cottage Door **22**
  Haymaker and Sleeping Girl 89, **90**
  Mr and Mrs Andrews 36, **37**, 64
gaze
  female 109
  male 89
    Haymaker and Sleeping Girl 90
gender
  differences, landscape perceptions 3, 4, 15, 18
  identity, and landscape 43
Genette, Gerard 85, 95, 97, 106
geography
  aesthetic ix, 3, 20, 23, 55, 97–8
  JA's interest in 3, 68
  of *Persuasion* 83–102
  psychic 92, 96
Gilbert, Sandra M. 86
Gilpin, William 5, 6, 27, 72
Gubar, Susan 86

habitat theory
  in 'Catharine – or the Bower' 87
  in *Mansfield Park* 87
  in *Persuasion* 88, 94
heroines, in the landscape 15–16, 18, 42–4, 56, 59, 60, 63–4, 66, 99–101, 113
Herrle, Jeffrey 39
Heydt-Stevenson, Jill 6, 8, 28
Highbury 63, 64
  as 'enclave of civility' 78
Hill, Reginald 31
'home', meaning 18
Honan, Park 83
Hughes, George 3
Hunt, John Dixon 76, 81

'impertinent', in *Emma* 79, 80

Jackson, J.B. 79, 80, 81
Johnson, Claudia 7
Johnson, Samuel 7

Kaplan, Deborah, *Jane Austen among Women* 4, 42
Kent, William 25, 78

Kirkham, Margaret 7
Knight, Edward ix
Knight, Richard Payne 6
Kroeber, Karl 66

landscape
  Annie Proulx on 1–2, 11
  and behaviour 2
  definitions 4, 5
  edge-of-the-wood phenomenon 9, 21, 26, 29, 71, 91, 97, 101, 113
  and English patriotism 24
  in *Evelina* 17
  gender
    differences in perception 3, 4, 15, 18, 36
    identity 43
  in *Heart of Midlothian* 99–102
  heroines in 15–16, 18, 42–4, 56, 59, 60, 63–4, 66, 99–101, 113
  in JA
    'Amelia Webster' 34
    'Catharine – Or The Bower' 38–40
    Emma 75–82, 111–12
    'Evelyn' 35, 36
    'Frederic and Elfrida' 32–3
    'Jack and Alice' 33
    'Love and Freindship' 34–5
    Mansfield Park 66–74
    Northanger Abbey 8, 43–50, 112
    Persuasion 38, 83–99, 101
    Pride and Prejudice 56–60
    Sanditon 103–10
    Sense and Sensibility 8, 52–6
  male control of 33–4, 53, 66, 89–91
  in Margaret Atwood 2
  and memory 97
  as metaphor 101
  modern writings 114–15
  and oppositions 41
  as palimpsest 8, 15, 16, 23, 32, 40, 59, 85, 95–6, 97, 98
  perception, layers of 99
  symbolic 21, 23
  in *The Mysteries of Udolpho* 23, 25, 28–9
  threatening 18–20, 23–4, 42
  use by authors 1
landscape architects 25–6
Lewes, George 35, 111
limen, meaning 3
liminality
  in Charlotte Brontë 113

  in JA 9, 59, 69–70, 98, 102, 108, 115
  in Sir Walter Scott 101
London, setting for *Sense and Sensibility* 54–5
Lorraine, Tamsin 43
'Lucy'
  poems (Wordsworth) 10, 13 n1, 24, 33, 35, 52, 88
  significance of name 33
Lukàcs, Georg 99
Lyme Regis 3, 42, 102, 113
  Cobb xi–xii, 42, 74, 91–2, 96, 98
  fossils 96–7
  as place of memory 98
  seascape 96

McMaster, Juliet 31, 36
Mansfield Park 63, 64, 115
  as 'enclave of civility' 67, 68, 74
Meinig, D.W. 18
memory
  and landscape 97
  and Lyme Regis 98
  and metaphor 95
metaphor
  landscape as 101
  and memory 95
Moers, Ellen 87, 96
More, Hannah 11, 17, 96, 102, 114
  Strictures...Female Education 66, 83, 85–6, 92–3
Morris, Mary 114

'natural' in *Emma* 75, 76, 77, 78, 80
Nickerson, Sheila, *Disappearance: A Map* 114
Nokes, David xi

Olin, Laurie, *Across the Open Field* 105–6
Ortner, Sherry 4, 42

palimpsest, landscape as 8, 15, 16, 23, 32, 40, 59, 85, 95–6, 97, 98
Palmer, Samuel, *View from Rook's Hill, Kent* 50, **51**, 115
patriarchy, and space 4
Pemberley 56–7, 59, 82, 113, 115
  as Darcy 57
picturesque, the
  and feminism 8, 27–8
  and JA 28
  writers on 6–8

meaning 6
and tourism 27
picturesque views, Bath 43
Portsmouth, as zone of exposure 73
Poussin, Gaspard 25
Price, Uvedale 6
prospect/refuge zone 12, 21, 43, 87, 115
   in *Mansfield Park* 70
   in *Northanger Abbey* 45, 47
   in *Persuasion* 88, 96–7, 100
   in *Pride and Prejudice* 59
   in *Sense and Sensibility* 53–4
   see also zone of compromise; zone of exposure; zone of safety
Proulx, Annie
   Close Range 2
   on landscape 1–2, 11

Quarterly Review 111

Radcliffe, Ann 8, 9, 14
   The Mysteries of Udolpho 15, 16, 20, 23, 27, 28–9, 45
Repton, Humphrey 6, 25, 26, 44, 45, 76, 81, 109
   and Stoneleigh Abbey 77–8
   works
      'Hints for the Improvement of Ferne Hall' 46–7
      Mr. Repton's Opinion of the Aspects **46**
      Plans, Sketches... 78
Ringer, G. 59
Rosa, Salvator 25
Rose, Gillian, *Feminism and Geography* 4, 64, 65, 114
Ross, Marlon 35
Russell, Alison, *Crossing Boundaries* 114

'safe place' 10, 15, 20, 54, 59, 70, 72, 79
Sales, Roger
   on Pemberley 56–7
   works
      Closer to Home 36
      Jane Austen and Regency England 6
      Writers and Place in England 6, 7–8
Scott, Walter, Sir
   on *Emma* 111–12
   JA, comparison 83–4, 99–102
   liminality in 101

   works
      The Fortunes of Nigel 99
      Heart of Midlothian 9, 11, 85, 99–101
Selborne ix
Smith, Charlotte 36
Snyder, W.C. 28
Sopher, David 18
Southam, Brian 11, 35, 40
   on *Sanditon* 103 n1 110
space, and patriarchy 4
Spacks, Patricia, *The Female Imagination* 87
Sterne, Laurence, *Sentimental Journey* 71
Steventon xi
Stoneleigh Abbey, as 'enclave of civility' 78
Sublime, the 6, 25, 26
   in *The Mysteries of Udolpho* 27
Sweden, JA on 3

Tanner, Tony 55, 58, 64
Thacker, Christopher 26
   History of Gardens 32
Thomson, James, 'Castle of Indolence' 25
tourism, and the picturesque 27
Tristram, Philippa 57
   Living Space in Fact and Fiction 6

Vauxhall Gardens, in *Evelina* 19–20

White, Gilbert x
Wollstonecraft, Mary 7, 102
Wordsworth, William 35
   'Lucy' poems 10, 13 n1 24, 33, 35, 52, 88
   'Nutting' 88–9

zone of compromise
   in Atwood's 'Death by Landscape' 23
   concept 16, 21
   in *Evelina* 18, 19
   Gainsborough's *Cottage Door* as 21, **22**
zone of exposure
   Box Hill as 80
   Portsmouth as 73
   The Cobb, Lyme Regis as 92
zone of safety x, xii, 12, 14, 40, 43, 47, 55, 70, 72, 91, 103
   Barton Cottage 53
   Donwell Abbey 82
   Rook's Hill 50

An environmentally friendly book printed and bound in England by www.printondemand-worldwide.com

PEFC Certified

This product is from sustainably managed forests and controlled sources

PEFC/16-33-415   www.pefc.org

This book is made of chain-of-custody materials; FSC materials for the cover and PEFC materials for the text pages.